ORIENTEERING
in the
NATIONAL CURRICULUM

STAGES 1 to 3

Published 1998 by

HARVEYS
12-16 Main Street
Doune, Perthshire FK16 6BJ
Tel: 01786 841202
Fax: 01786 841098
E-mail: sales@harveymaps.co.uk

ISBN 1 85137 399 3

Acknowledgements

Alan Goodall
BOF Schools Officer for advice on QCA Recommendations and Assessment

Glynn Roberts
Head of the Birmingham Urban Outdoor Education Centre for providing educational perspectives on the use of city parks for orienteering and illustrating through the City of Birmingham Orienteering Club the potential for Club - School initiatives in an urban environment

Jan Goodall and Ormskirk C.E. Primary School
Illustrations on site 'string orienteering'

Map illustrations reproduced with permission of the King Edward Foundation, Wrekin Orienteering Club, Walton Chasers, Central Regional Council. Copyright reserved

Lesson plan illustrations: Ian Whalley

Cover photos: Marlene Palmer & Ormskirk C.E. Primary School

THE AUTHORS

CAROL McNEILL

Carol McNeill's career in orienteering has parallelled that of the development of the sport in Britain. Her 7th place in the World Championships in Finland in 1979 is still one of Britain's highest individual placings at this level. She won the World Veteran Women's Championship in Norway in 1986 and again in Scotland in 1994.

She has developed and spread her wide coaching experience and technical expertise at every level from grass roots to elite for 20 years, acting as Senior Squad Coaching Co-ordinator, coach to International teams, international selector and tutor to many coaching courses at home and abroad, including an extended period in Western Australia developing orienteering at schools and grass roots levels.

As a teacher of Physical Education in a Lake District school she has unrivalled experience in intra and extra curricular orienteering with children of all ages, and has translated her ideas into many publications and articles. She is co-author of 'Teaching Orienteering', 'Start Orienteering' and the International Orienteering Federation's 'Orienteering for the Young'. Her book 'Orienteering - Skills of the Game' is a best seller world wide.

JIM MARTLAND

Jim Martland is Director of the NCF/Liverpool University Research Project into Developing Children's Navigational Skills is involved in new findings on teaching and developing compass skills and to use and adapt National Curriculum analyses and assessment models provided for a Practical Guide into Orienteering in the National Curriculum Key Stages 1 and 2.

PETER PALMER

Before becoming the British Orienteering Federation's first director of Coaching, Peter Palmer taught in Secondary Schools of all types for 30 years. He is now a governor of two schools and member of the curriculum committees, and is still active with wife Marlene in developing junior orienteering at national, regional and local levels.

At various times during the past twenty years he has chaired BOF Schools' and Coaching Committees, founded and organised the National Junior Squad from which most of Britain's current crop of orienteers have emerged, and run national and international courses on junior and grass roots orienteering development. These include three International Orienteering Federation 'Clinics' in Sweden, as well as courses for teachers and coaches in Canada, Bulgaria, Hong Kong and Australia. He also has wide experience in planning and organising major national championships and international competitions.

He edited the current BOF 'Complete orienteering manual for Coaches'. Other publications include 'The Coaching Collection' (with Jim Martland), 'Orienteering: Pathways to Excellence', the IOF's 'Orienteering for the Young' (with Carol McNeill and Tom Renfrew). He was elected a Fellow of the Royal Institute of Navigation for services to navigational education.

He brings a wealth of theoretical and practical ideas and insight to the pages which follow.

Contents

Foreword

Orienteering with young people has been a central theme of my life for 30 years. I have always seen education as opening windows to new experiences and helping children to come to terms with the world outside school. Orienteering does just that.

My first orienteering ventures with Surrey school children in the early 1960's relied on black and white photocopies of Ordnance Survey maps and 'canvas bucket' type control markers made by a needlework class. The word 'orienteering' meant nothing to the majority of school children. Thirty years later we have accurate 5 colour maps specially made for orienteering, permanent courses and well-tried teaching schemes which avoid the traumas of children getting badly lost - but the basic magic remains the same. The young orienteer has to negotiate a natural wilderness relying on his or her own intelligence, physique, map-reading skills and compass. Usually the course cannot be easily mastered by direct assault and the competitor has to contour round hillsides, skirt bogs or thickets and decide upon the best path routes. If all goes well, the result is the exquisite thrill of sighting the small orange and white marker through the trees, an experience which touches the David Livingstone in all of us.

This publication offers teachers sufficient information and ideas both to open up the magic for their pupils and at the same time to use orienteering as a practical means for developing skills across the National Curriculum.

Most of my own teaching and coaching experience has been with youngsters in the 11 to 18 age group but I can say with confidence that sound teaching along the lines suggested in this book will lead younger as well as older pupils into a rich vein of educational experience. The English National Curriculum for Physical Education, Geography and Mathematics offers many opportunities for children to experience the adventurous potential of orienteering in the school locality as well as to explore wider dimensions of mapping, course planning and performance improvement. Many too, I hope, will be motivated to enjoy competition and friendships in the wider orienteering world. Others will be encouraged to enjoy the countryside with confidence and safety.

For many children today, television, the car and the pressures of an acquisitive society have subordinated the natural world to a backcloth for a sedentary existence. Dangerous urban environments no longer allow children to play the free-range games they enjoyed in the past. As well as teaching important life skills and delivering curriculum attainment targets as described in the pages which follow, orienteering has the potential to bring back excitement, energy and adventure into many restricted young lives.

The British Orienteering Federation is to be congratulated on its continuing support for this imaginative venture.

Peter Palmer
Coaching Director of the British Orienteering Federation from 1986 to 1992 and Fellow of the Royal Institute of Navigation

PREFACE

Reshaping 'Orienteering in the National Curriculum' to cover changes in the Curriculum since 1992 has been a difficult task. Ron Dearing optimistically stated after implementing his revised curriculum for Key Stages 1-3 in 1995 that no major changes would be made to the National Curriculum for 5 years from 1995. This has not been the case.

Successive government revisions have given greater emphasis to the core subjects of English, Maths and Science. The introduction of literacy and numeracy hours has further squeezed the time available for subjects like Art, Music and PE, as well as for the study of cross curricular themes.

Even within the PE curriculum a Qualifications and Curriculum Authority document published in June 1998 states that the 'Secretary of State has proposed that for two years from September 1998 schools have only to have regard to the teaching of physical education. This means that the current statutory requirement to teach the full programme of study will be lifted'. The implication of this will be that outdoor and adventurous activities will have to fight hard for a place in PE in competition with games, gymnastic activities and dance.

The process of slimming down the English National Curriculum may therefore continue. We can only say at this stage that, although it will remain in a state of flux, the orienteering analysis and advice given in this book will remain valid.

For the sake of clarity and coherence, we will start by summarising the Dearing changes and other developments with their implications for orienteering within the curriculum. They will be reflected in the revision which follows. Other additions to the first edition have also been made to bring this second edition into line with current teaching and coaching practice for orienteering.

We hope that the new book receives the same enthusiastic reception from teachers as the first publication.

THE DEARING CHANGES AND THEIR IMPLICATIONS

In April 1993, the Secretary of State for Education invited Sir Ron Dearing to review the structure, manageability and assessment arrangements of the National Curriculum. After wide consultations the following suggestions were made:

1
The National Curriculum should be slimmed down and its prescriptiveness reduced, thereby increasing scope for teachers' professional judgement.

2
Time should be released which schools could use at their discretion - the equivalent of one day per week at Key Stages 1 to 3.

3
Any reductions should be concentrated on subjects other than English, Maths and Science.

4
Flexibility and choice should be increased at Key Stage 4.

5
Assessment and administration loads should be significantly reduced.

The School Curriculum and Assessment Authority's final recommendations on the revised National Curriculum were accepted by the Secretary of State in November 1994 and implementation was started from August 1995. The revised curriculum involved some adjustment of the place that orienteering could take in Physical Education, Geography and Maths, which is reflected in this book.

It should be pointed out that the Lesson Plans in both of the two existing orienteering curriculum books, at Key Stages 1 & 2 and at Key Stages 3 & 4, remain as relevant and up-to-date as when written. Similarly, despite changes to terminology and content within Programmes of Study, all the orienteering examples given in the two books can be applied just as appropriately to the new structure.

OVERVIEW

Let us now look at the new post-Dearing Curriculum, first in general terms, then as specific to the three main 'orienteering subjects' of Physical Education, Geography and Maths. As with the 'old' National Curriculum, **the new structure is a consistent one**:

1
There are common requirements covering access to the curriculum, use of language and applications of information technology across the curriculum.

2
Programmes of Study provide the basis for planning and teaching the curriculum and they are set out by Key Stage.

3
Attainment Targets are provided for making judgements on pupils' progress.

4
Level Descriptions replace Statements of Attainment. The ten-level scale has been reduced to eight, plus a level of exceptional performance. It applies only to Key Stages 1, 2 and 3.

5
The function of the Level Descriptions is to assist in making judgements on pupil perform-

ance. They indicate the type and range of performance which pupils working at a particular level should demonstrate.

6
In Physical Education (as in Art and Music), End of Key Stage **Descriptions** now replace End of Key Stage *Statements*. These describe the types and range of performance which most pupils should demonstrate at the end of each Key Stage. In broad terms, the Key Stage 1 Description equates to Level 2; Key Stage 2 to level 4; and Key Stage 3 to levels 5/6.

7
To encourage high expectations, a Description of Performance above Level 8 has been added to each Attainment Target to help teachers identify exceptional achievement. For the same reason there is an additional description at Key Stage 4 in Physical Education.

8
The assessment load has been much reduced. Even in English, Maths and Science where teacher assessment will be statutory at the end of each Key Stage from 1997, detailed records related to Statements of Attainment are no longer demanded. Decisions about recording progress are now seen as professional matters for schools to consider in the context of pupils' needs and the legal compulsion to report to parents what their children have achieved in the curriculum.

9
How and in what depth to teach the material and in what subject order is for schools to decide. Depth of treatment of aspects of subjects is now left to the professional judgement of teachers.

10
Examples shown in the Programmes of Study can be used at the discretion of schools.

11
At Key Stage 4, schools have been given increased flexibility to develop courses appropriate to pupils' aptitudes and needs. The minimum statutory National Curriculum requirement in English maintained schools at Key Stage 4 still includes Maths and PE but Geography now becomes optional.

The revised Dearing curriculum came into force:
1st August 1995: Key Stages 1-3 for all years,
1st August 1996: Key Stage 4 for year 10
1st August 1997: Key Stage 4 for year 11

ORIENTEERING IN THE CURRICULUM

From this survey some implications for orienteering in the curriculum become obvious. In particular the assessment sections in "Orienteering in the National Curriculum", particularly at Key Stage 1 and 2, are now over prescriptive. Chapter 6 in "Key Stages 3 & 4 in the National Curriculum" comments that assessment of orienteering activity should not be complex or time consuming and that evaluation and asessment should be part of a professional approach to the whole learning progress in co-operation with pupils and other teachers. This fits very well with the new Dearing approach for all Key Stages. The basic approach to orienteering assessment remains as described, but the tick-and-cross approach needs to be related more closely to the importance of the activity in the total subject scheme. It might have to be toned down to cut out excessive paper work and time on what is a means to learning rather than an end.

ORIENTEERING AND SPECIFIC SUBJECTS IN THE CURRICULUM

Now we will look at the place of orienteering in specific subject areas of the revised curriculum. As already described, the new National Curriculum is a much slimmer document. Although some material in some subjects has been transferred from one key stage to another there is very little new material. It is much less prescriptive and leaves much more to the individual teacher. The information and advice in "Orienteering in the National Curriculum" is still wholly applicable and relevant to the subject areas of Physical Education, Geography and Maths as identified, but within the new spirit of Dearing teachers will have to use professional judgement and imagination in applying orienteering within the new flexible structure.

GEOGRAPHY

We will start with **Geography** because of the three 'orienteering areas' in the curriculum, it has changed most. It is now much simplified and far less prescriptive.

1 Progression between Key Stages is now more clearly defined. The importance of enquiry skills is stressed at each Key Stage and locational knowledge requirements are integrated into

the general requirements and skills section of each Key Stage. The five previous Attainment Targets are replaced by one, which emphasises the integration of skills, places and themes within geography.

2 The prescribed content in all three Key Stages has been substantially reduced and duplication with science has been removed.

3 The content is not related to levels. It is left up to schools to develop different schemes of work suited to pupils' needs. The Level Descriptions indicate how pupils may progress in components of the subject such as enquiry skills or knowledge and understanding of places.

Key stage 1
Pupils now have to study two places (the school locality and a contrasting locality) and one theme (environmental quality). Some wider locational knowledge and a range of geographical skills, like making maps and following directions, are also required. Orienteering obviously can have a direct input here.

Key stage 2
Pupils have to study three places and four themes, ranging from local to national. Wider locational knowledge and a greater range of skills are required than at Key Stage 1 - where orienteering can again make a significant contribution.

Key stage 3

There is much greater scope for teacher choice in selecting places of study and therefore much less prescription.

The requirement now is for two places (contrasting countries) and nine themes across a range of skills from local to global. Wide locational knowledge and geographical skills make the orienteering examples given in the curriculum books just as applicable as before.

Geography is no longer a compulsory subject at Key Stage 4.

MATHEMATICS

Key Stage 1

The number of Attainment Targets has been reduced from five to three:

Using and Applying Mathematics
Number
Shape and Space

Key Stages 2 and 3

The number of Attainment Targets has been reduced from five to four:

Using and Applying Mathematics
Number
Shape and Space
Handling Data

In addition

• Key Stage Programmes of Study replace Programmes of Study set out by level.

• There are separate Key Stage 1 and Key Stage 2 Programmes of Study.

• A joint programme for Key Stage 3 and 4 brings together material appropriate to each of these Key Stages.

• Further material which is specified separately for Key Stage 4 has no orienteering connection.

The orienteering applications to Maths in the two curriculum books are little affected by these changes.

PHYSICAL EDUCATION

In general terms, the new curriculum offers the same opportunities for orienteering as the old - except at Key Stage 1 where outdoor and adventurous activities and athletic activity no longer appear as compulsory elements.

However, the increased accent on games and greater choice now offered to teachers means that orienteering, like other outdoor activities, will have to 'fight its corner' hard.

The changes are as follows:

• The four sections in the current Programme of Study have been reduced to three.

• The current general requirements have been slimmed and references to teaching methodology have been deleted.

• References to health related exercise have been placed in the introductory requirements to each Key Stage.

Key Stage 1

The number of areas of activity has been reduced from five to three (games, gymnastic activities and dance) with swimming as a fourth optional activity.

Key Stage 2

All areas of activity have been slimmed down apart from games. Swimming has been thinned down with some content moved to Key Stage 3.

Greater weighting has been accorded to games, gymnastic activities and dance as against athletic activities, outdoor and adventurous activities and swimming.

Key stage 3

Reduction has been achieved by splitting the areas of activity in two. Breadth and balance

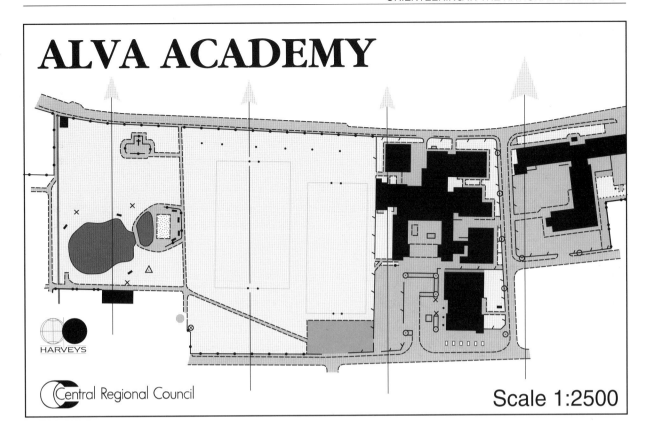

ALVA ACADEMY

HARVEYS

Central Regional Council

Scale 1:2500

have been preserved by requiring pupils to pursue four areas of activity: two as full units and two has half units. Games must be included as a full area of activity for each year of the Key Stage.

The inclusion of swimming as an area of activity increases choice.

Key stage 4
Swimming is included to give continuity from Key Stage 3. One of the two chosen activities must be a game,

Within **Outdoor and Adventurous and Athletic Activities** the emphasis given to activity on and off site, self evaluation, skill acquisition, problem solving, safety and creating challenges for others, means that orienteering clearly retains the place defined for it in "Orienteering in the National Curriculum" at all key stages from 1 to 4. Teachers can still exercise professional choice in including orienteering in the school curriculum at Key Stage 1 as a cross curriculur activity ideally suited to developing geographical, mathematical and PE skills.

The **Programmes of Study** and **Assessment** sections in this second edition book have been completely rewritten to encompass all these changes.

Peter Palmer
July 1998

1 Introduction

Orienteering is basically a simple sport in which competitors navigate round a series of checkpoints using a large scale map and sometimes a compass. The kit is simple - just sensible outdoor clothes, a pair of trainers with 'grip' and a clear polythene bag to use as a map case. Although the fastest back wins, navigat-ional skills are more important than running speed and the competition is often more with self than others.

Like all sports, success demands a mastery of basic skills - map orientation, pacing, distance judgement, etc - but, unlike many sports, orienteering can take a variety of forms. It can be performed recreationally or competitively by all ages and levels of technical and physical ability. Whether point-to-point, score, line, relay or a 'trail' event, it still combines the essential elements of navigation, decision making and activity - and above all, remains fun.

It can take place in the classroom, in school grounds, or in woodland. Courses can take a couple of hours or a few minutes and competitors can walk, run, ride a mountain bike or even paddle a canoe if the opportunity exists. The basic criteria are that maps must be large scale and accurate, the control points must be identifiable by skill and not luck, and the emphasis in course planning should be on following a chosen route successfully and not in looking for a hidden control marker. Orienteering can be a treasure hunt only if the treasure is located solely by applied skill. Experience shows that children introduced to the sport by a positive system which builds on confidence are much more likely to continue than those haunted by fears of getting lost.

Orienteering started in Sweden about 80 years ago. Today, Scandinavian events attract many thousands of participants and "orienteering and the outdoor life" is a compulsory element within the Swedish National Curriculum. In a large country of which four-fifths is forest, it is important that its citizens can find their way about confidently, particularly during the summer months when many Swedes emerge from winter 'hibernation' to enjoy the countryside. Free access to the countryside

(Allemansrätt) is every citizen's birthright, and a healthy lifestyle means lower health bills.

The sport came to Britain in the late 1950's. Since then it has grown steadily, and now there is a full programme of events across the country most weekends. Thousands of children have been introduced to its various dimensions through Outdoor Education schemes and intra- and extra-curricular activities in individual schools. The British Schools Championships regularly attract well over a thousand entrants from all over the UK. The sport is controlled and governed by the British Orienteering Federation.

There are already well-tried systems for progressing children's orienteering from classroom to campus and local park. The practical emphasis on map reading and route finding within the Geography National Curriculum and the inclusion of Outdoor Adventure activities in the PE Curriculum have given a new dimension to educational orienteering. Nor are these the only curricular areas where orienteering has direct relevance. Because it involves map scales, direction and measurement, mathematics comes into the picture, while problem-solving brings in personal education, communication and language. The countryside introduces the environment, new locations mean adventure, while the organisation of orienteering activities and provision of equipment involve design and technology. The guide which follows explores all these cross-curricular links as well as identifying the key areas of orienteering input.

Orienteering thus offers a creative but inexpensive outdoor activity on the school site or close by, but understandably, many busy teachers see it as complicated, time-consuming and difficult to set up. This book sets out to allay those fears by relating orienteering activities to identified curriculum areas and by giving clear guidance on how to plan lessons and assess results, as well as providing resource information and references to more detailed publications. It concentrates on effective use of the immediate school environment and, while prescriptive in approach, it leaves teachers free to adapt the lesson plans to individual schemes of work or personal areas of interest. It pursues, step by step, the well researched orienteering teaching system of orientated map (by compass or ground), the following of 'line feature' routes, and progression from classroom to the wider world.

Teachers are free to decide when and how to introduce specific activities or to assess how much weight to give to competitive activity as against group work, map-making or environmental interest. Similarly, teachers themselves can decide how far to involve children in making basic equipment such as control markers and how far to use commercial suppliers. As part of a community studies project, one school recently designed and set up a permanent course with a newly drawn map and fixed control posts on a disused mining site. The mapping, construction and negotiation involved

Geography, Maths, Technology, Environmental Studies, Social Education, Language and some local history, while physical fitness was called for in the competition organised for the official opening.

The arrangement of this guide is straightforward. It is intended for practising teachers and instructors in outdoor education centres and it therefore assumes a working knowledge of the National Curriculum. It concentrates upon Key Stages 1 and 2, although much of what is described and recommended applies equally well at Key Stage 3.

This introduction is followed by an examination of areas within the National Curriculum where there are clear opportunities to use orienteering activities within study programmes. It then moves on to provide a series of practical ideas and lesson plans that are related to specific areas. A framework of assessment suggests ways of recording progress in simple user-friendly ways. Chapters that follow suggest extensions beyond school for those teachers or children who wish to pursue their interest further. The guide concludes with appendices containing sample maps and resource information. Above all, it is intended to provide teachers with simple, useful information on how to use orienteering realistically as a practical vehicle for delivering Attainment Targets within the National Curriculum.

Finally, whichever path you take through the orienteering 'forest', we hope that, you will enjoy the pleasure of seeing children grow in self-confidence and awareness as they develop their interest in this fascinating activity. We can guarantee that, whatever your objectives at the start of your orienteering journey into the National Curriculum, you will explore many byways and diversions en route that would not have presented themselves at the start.

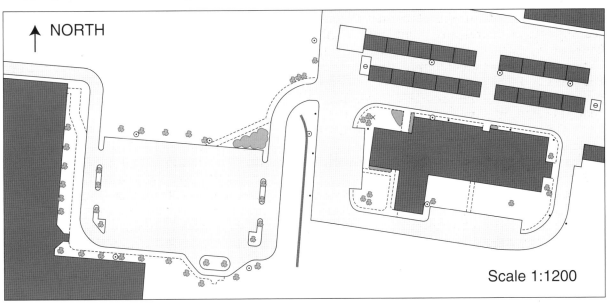

NORTH

Scale 1:1200

2 How Orienteering relates to the National Curriculum

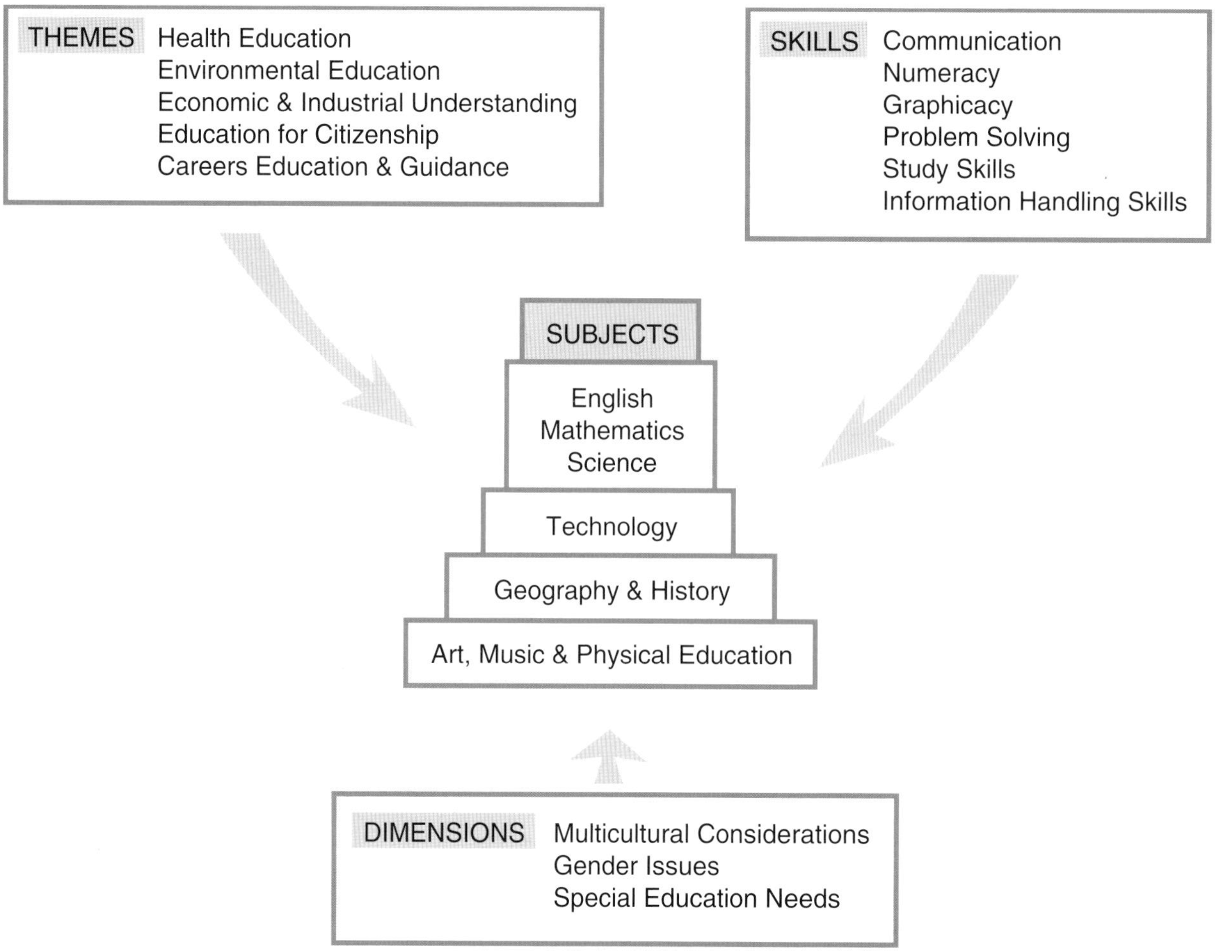

THEMES	Health Education
	Environmental Education
	Economic & Industrial Understanding
	Education for Citizenship
	Careers Education & Guidance

SKILLS	Communication
	Numeracy
	Graphicacy
	Problem Solving
	Study Skills
	Information Handling Skills

SUBJECTS

English
Mathematics
Science

Technology

Geography & History

Art, Music & Physical Education

DIMENSIONS	Multicultural Considerations
	Gender Issues
	Special Education Needs

Aspects of the National Curriculum

INTRODUCTION

In this chapter we show how different forms of orienteering relate to the National Curriculum. We discuss how involvement in small scale events draws the different subject areas together into a cohesive project which not only teaches facts, skills and knowledge but also inculcates positive attitudes and values. The chapter concludes with a rationale for teaching orienteering, and raises questions to be addressed as a form of assessment, points which are followed up in Chapter 5.

ASPECTS OF THE NATIONAL CURRICULUM

The National Curriculum consists of a number of subjects, though not all are given equal weight. The core reflects the 'old basics' of mathematics and English, to which has been added the relatively new subject (for primary schools) of science. Technology forms a second tier with geography and history adding the third layer. Art, music and physical education complete the steps.

It presents an adventure activity on the school's doorstep

It's real problem solving

It's useful

It's challenging

It develops life skills

It's a good leisure activity

It opens children's horizons to a new sport

It's decision making

It's enjoyable

It's fun

It's motivating

It builds self confidence and independence

It's map and compass

Everyone can do it

It gives children confidence to find their way

It provides purpose and relevance to learning

It builds health and fitness in an individual way

It uses the real world rather than exercises in books

It links mathematics and geography

It gets you out of the classroom

It gets children talking

It enables children to observe their environment

It answers PE and Outdoor Adventure Education cost effectively

What teachers say about orienteering as a topic for delivering the National Curriculum

However, subject knowledge alone cannot deliver the National Curriculum. Three cross-curricular elements have been added in an attempt to tie the basic curriculum together. These three elements are termed skills, dimensions and themes and, though non-statutory, they cover important areas of knowledge and understanding and are intended to permeate the whole curriculum.

The skills were originally called 'competencies' and include communication, numeracy and graphicacy skills, problem solving, information handling and study skills. Themes, such as health education, environmental education and citizenship, show how close links can be made with subjects, while the dimensions relate to personal and social education as well as addressing bias and discrimination.

THEORY INTO ACTION

The basic challenge for the busy primary teacher is that of translating the theory of the National Curriculum into action. Although the subjects themselves may be seen as separate entities, the Programmes of Study do overlap.

Furthermore, the subject hierarchy and associated assessment tasks could severely limit the time available for subjects such as history and geography. Time constraints can be alleviated by combining areas of the curriculum, but the separate Programmes of Study in their individually coloured ring binders neither assist nor motivate teachers to draw the necessary threads and connections which exist between them.

It is also true that the statements to be covered can appear prescriptive and complex, requiring specialist knowledge. Although the Programmes of Study should not be seen as 'set in stone', or rigidly matched to the age and needs of every child, some teachers understandably find it difficult to deliver the curriculum effectively, particularly from a cross-curricular perspective.

This need not be the case, and a study of orienteering can help to link core and foundation subjects and embrace skills, themes and dimensions. Reactions from teachers who have tried the materials provides many positive comments about the value of orienteering. How does this come about?

FINDING THE WAY

Orienteering is a sport in which a map and compass are used to decide on a route to a precise destination, at which there is a control marker. The skills involved are similar in many ways to those used in everyday life when using a map, whether walking or driving. A clearer understanding of the techniques involved will allow children and adults to become more confident in their use of maps.

The challenge of orienteering is that of solving the route choice problem efficiently and speedily in order to reach the precise destination (the control marker). The practical value of a knowledge of map and compass skills rapidly becomes apparent. It is not about learning cardinal points, symbols or grid references for their own sake, but more about relating the map and compass to the terrain and in turn, noticing features on the ground which can be located on the map. Orienteering thus uses two important tools, the map and the compass, knowledge of which will be useful in fieldwork, both in the local environment and in the wider world.

So where do we start? First with a simple map of the classroom, hall, gymnasium, playground, school field or local park. The map should be clear, large scale and the features on it should be correct in the depiction of size and relationship to each other.

With the help of a school plan, drawing film and careful penwork a teacher can prepare their own map, but there are now many map suppliers which can produce accurate coloured school site maps relatively cheaply. The OCAD computer programme also makes it possible now to draw the map and store it on the school computer, which makes updating very easy. It is possible to involve young pupils in drawing and updating maps on computer. See Appendix E.

A good site map, with if possible attendant park maps, is the key to successful schools orienteering.

Let us assume for the moment that the pupil understands the concept of a map, can recognise plan view and understands the notion of a key. What questions then confront the young navigator? As they arise, consider not only their importance but also whether they are covered by conventional mapwork teaching and exercises. The questions centre around four important ideas: orientation, route choice, map contact and location.

Key questions to ask yourself:
ORIENTATION:
Is the map the right way round?
Does the map match the ground?
How can I use landmarks to set the map?
How do I use the compass to set the map?
Note: You can always set a map with a compass, but only sometimes by using landmarks.

ROUTE CHOICE:
Where am I now?
Can I find this point on the map?
Where am I going?
Which way can I go?
Are there any other possible routes?
Are there obstacles or difficulties on my route?
Which route is shortest?
Which route is quickest?
Which route is easiest?
Which route is best?
How far is it?
How long will I take?
In which direction do I set off?

STAYING ON ROUTE:
How do I know I'm still on route?
What will I notice and check off on my route?
How will I know when I'm near my destination?
How can I keep a check on my position?
What skills do I need to do all this well?

ON ARRIVAL:
Did my plan work out in action?
Did I find the destination precisely?
Was the route a good one?
Did I meet unexpected problems?
Could my route have been simpler or quicker?

Was I hesitant or confident?
Did I need to keep checking the map?
Did I map read accurately?
Did I use the compass?
Did I take note of distance?
How long did I take?
How pleased was I with my performance?

Can the answers to these important questions be located within the National Curriculum at Key Stages 1 and 2?

The answer is yes. Principally, the activities match skills in the geography programmes of study. For example, using maps of routes and small areas, interpreting symbols, directional skills, describing location, identifying features and using a compass. Similarly, the activities relate to the use and application of mathematics (AT1) and to Shape and Space (AT3), as many key concepts such as distance, direction, location, shape, scale, links and networks are shared with geography.

The sport of orienteering readily fits into outdoor and adventurous education, while its specific techniques can form games and athletic activity. Finally, after any act of navigation or wayfinding you inevitably talk to others about the experience. The ability to recall and describe your route, and how you travelled along it, provide opportunities for English.

GEOGRAPHY
Geographical Skills
    (i) The use of maps
    (ii) Fieldwork techniques
Places
Thematic Studies

MATHEMATICS
AT1 Using and applying mathematics
        (i) in practical tasks
        (ii) real life problem solving
AT3 Shape, Space and Measures
        (i) use measurement and location
            in the study of space

ORIENTEERING:
ROUTE PROBLEM SOLVING
"FINDING YOUR WAY"

Specific requirements:
    (i) Games
    (ii) Athletic activity
    (iii) Outdoor and adventurous activities
General requirement:
    Physical activity
PHYSICAL EDUCATION

AT1 Speaking and listening
AT3 Writing

ENGLISH

The Skills of Orienteering and Links with Core and Foundation Subjects

TYPES OF ORIENTEERING

One of the values of orienteering is that it can take many forms. The same familiar area can be used repeatedly to extend the range of skills and experience while providing a secure setting for the pupil, and thus raising confidence. In our experience children soon begin to want to run, rather than walk, and so competition, both against yourself and others, becomes a natural extension.

Orienteering is a sport of physical and mental challenge, usually undertaken on an individual basis, but there are also opportunities for group activities and team events. The different forms of orienteering set out here form a whole succession and range of exercises to practice and develop map and compass skills within the school grounds.

POINT TO POINT ORIENTEERING

In the basic competitive form of orienteering, a course is completed by visiting a number of control points in a set order. The winner is the person who correctly completes the course in the shortest time. Courses can be circular or crossover in design.

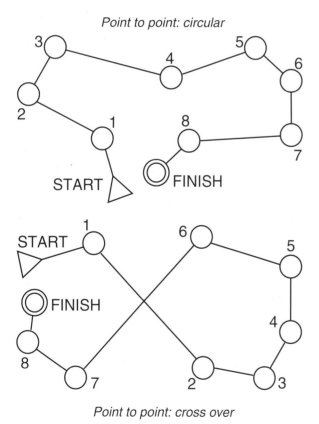

Point to point: circular

Point to point: cross over

SCORE ORIENTEERING

In score events, a large number of controls are set out and each is given a points value, depending on degree of difficulty and distance from the start. A set time is given to collect as

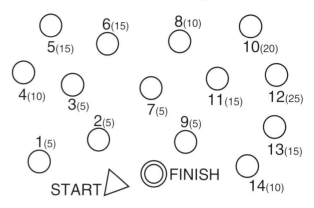

Score orienteering

many control points as possible, with a scale of penalty points being deducted for late return.

In team score events, teams of two, three or four work together to collect the controls. Decisions have to be made within the time allocation as to who goes for which controls. Again, a set time limit is given and there are penalties for being late back.

RELAY ORIENTEERING

Relays are fun and exert time pressure as well as team responsibility on competitors. Teams are normally of three, and the map is used as a type of baton. There are several variations on how the courses can be set out. In some events, 'common controls' are used on all courses, to increase interest for both competitors and spectators, as this enables race progress to be judged.

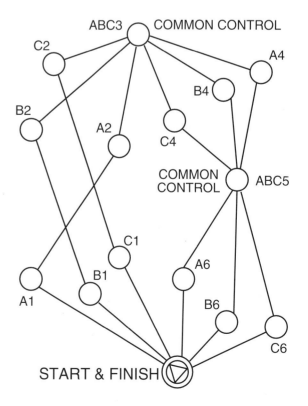

Relay orienteering

Do they...
Observe features, note what is where?
Discuss what the place is like?
Discuss direction, location, scale?
Discuss reaction to a place?
Think - why is this place like this?
Respond to a place?
Respond actively?

GEOGRAPHY
Geographical Skills
   (i) The use of maps
   (ii) Fieldwork techniques
Places
Thematic Studies

Do they...   develop the ability to tackle problems?
Use mathematics effectively?
Work independently? Work collaboratively?
Work as a team? Evaluate solutions?
Use mathematical tools (compass) with confidence?
Estimate results in advance?
Persevere?
Are they.. motivated
to have a go?
Accurate?
Systematic?
Willing to check?

MATHEMATICS
AT1 Using and applying mathematics
   (i) in practical tasks
   (ii) real life problem solving
AT3 Shape, Space and Measures
   (i) Use measurement and location
      in the study of space

ORIENTEERING:
ROUTE PROBLEM SOLVING
"FINDING YOUR WAY"

Do they...
Follow rules?
Respond readily
  to instructions?
Become aware of
  the effect of their
  actions on
  (a) others (b) the environment?
Observe fair play, honest competition?
Act in a sporting manner?
Cope with success and failure?
Learn skills and practise?
Learn to evaluate their initial attempts and
  decide how to modify subsequent attempts?

Specific requirements:
   (i) Games
   (ii) Athletic activity
   (iii) Outdoor and adventurous activities
General requirement:
   Physical activity
PHYSICAL EDUCATION

AT1 Speaking and listening
AT3 Writing

ENGLISH

Do they...   Listen:
hear explanations,
instructions,
questions and
answers?

Talk:
make predictions,
ask questions,
talk through difficulties,
report outcomes, use relevant language?

Reflect:
upon outcomes, strategies and actions?

Observing children orienteering: personal reactions, attitudes and qualities

Many practices and activities can be used in preparation for the above variations. We have set out a suggested sequence of lesson plans in Chapter 4.

Collaborative efforts under time and distance pressure present real challenges and so orienteering can be used to see not only whether the navigational problems are solved, but also how they are solved.

The diagram *Observing children orienteering* (above) shows statements from the non-statutory guidance of the National Curriculum in Geography, English, Mathematics and PE. It has been designed to provide a list of questions which can be foremost in the teacher's mind when observing the children at work either individually or collaboratively.

The statements contain elements which cohesive schemes of work should possess together with the qualities, attitudes and values to be generated. There is considerable overlap between subjects, but equally there are distinctions. Mathematics illustrates the skills and attitudes required in problem-solving while physical education emphasises playing your part and obeying rules. Both subjects encourage practice and reflection, which is also apparent in the discussion element of English.

Geography is not just a study of place but also how you react to it, not just features on maps and photographs but how you feel about being there. To orienteer, first within the school grounds and then in wider areas, can lead to an examination of how you feel about measures of security, the enjoyment of success, the feeling of failure, the disappointment of underachievement or the general wellbeing of having played your part within a particular context. All these affect our understanding of place.

3   Programmes of study

MATHEMATICS
AND ORIENTEERING IN THE NATIONAL CURRICULUM

USING AND APPLYING MATHEMATICS (ATTAINMENT TARGET 1)

PROGRAMME OF STUDY Pupils should engage in activities which involve:	STATEMENT OF ATTAINMENT Pupils should be able to:	EXAMPLES IN ORIENTEERING Pupils could:
LEVEL 1		
• using mathematics for a practical task • talking about their work and asking questions	• use mathematics as an integral part of practical classroom tasks • talk about their own work and respond to questions • make predictions, etc.	• count models used for desk top plans • discuss shapes of models • talk about size of shapes used as symbols for models or apparatus • make and put out a control marker
LEVEL 2		
• asking and responding to questions, eg "What would happen if ...? Why ...?"	• talk about work using appropriate mathematical language • respond appropriately to the question "What would happen if ...?"	• discuss relationship of child to desk top models depending on which side they look at it. The house is in front of the wall, the tree is beside the house ..
LEVEL 3		
• explaining work and recording findings systematically	• find ways of overcoming difficulties in problem solving • use or interpret appropriate mathematical terms and aspects of everyday language in a precise way	• learn how to travel on a route • record letters from numbered orienteering control markers
LEVEL 4		
• selecting the materials and the mathematics to use for a task when the information leaves opportunities for choice and for planning work methodically • recording findings and presenting them in oral, written or visual form	• identify and obtain information necessary to solve problems • interpret situations mathematically, using appropriate symbols or diagrams • make generalisations	• discuss what information is needed to find a control • draw classroom or playground maps to scale • time a competition and put the results in correct order • generate strategies for point to point and score events
LEVEL 5		
• selecting the materials and the mathematics to use for a task; checking there is sufficient information; working methodically and reviewing progress • breaking tasks into smaller, more manageable sections • interpreting mathematical information presented in oral, written or visual form	• carry through a task by breaking it down into smaller, more manageable sections • interpret information presented in a variety of mathematical forms • make a generalisation and test it	• plan a short course • solve a route choice problem • decide on score values for control points in score orienteering • discuss the use of scale for plans and maps • discuss how it feels to cover a specific distance on the ground measured from the map • test that the most direct route is not always the quickest • test strategies for aiming off

MATHEMATICS
AND ORIENTEERING IN THE NATIONAL CURRICULUM

NUMBER (ATTAINMENT TARGET 2)

PROGRAMME OF STUDY *Pupils should engage in activities which involve:*	STATEMENT OF ATTAINMENT *Pupils should be able to:*	EXAMPLES IN ORIENTEERING *Pupils could:*
LEVEL 1		
• counting, reading, writing and ordering numbers to at least 10 • learning that the size of a set is given by the last number in the count • understanding language associated with number, e.g. 'more', 'fewer', 'same' • understanding conservation of number • making a sensible estimate of a number of objects up to 10 • using addition and subtraction, with numbers no greater that 10, in the context of real objects	• use number in the context of the classroom and school • add and subtract using a small number of objects	• count control points • count models on apparatus • find 3 controls from 5 • select a number of models to draw a desk top plan
LEVEL 2		
• knowing and using addition and subtraction facts up to 100 • reading, writing, ordering numbers to at least 100; using the knowledge that the 10s digit indicates the number of 10s • solving whole-number problems involving addition and subtraction, including money • using non-standard measures in length, area, capacity, weight and time; comparing objects and events and recognising the need for standard units	• demonstrate that they know and can use number facts, including addition and subtraction • solve whole-number problems involving addition and subtraction • identify halves and quarters • recognise the need for standard units of measurement	• calculate the maximum points possible in a score event • discuss how drawing objects to scale solves the problem of not being able to accommodate them (life-size) on a sheet of paper • relate rotation to cardinal points • discuss rotation and identify features on half and quarter rotations
LEVEL 3		
• reading, writing and ordering numbers up to at least 1000, and using the knowledge that the position of a digit indicates its value • learning and using addition and subtraction facts to 20 (including zero) • learning and using multiplication facts up to 5 x 5 and all those in the 2, 5 and 10 multiplication tables • making estimates based on familiar units • recognising that the first digit is the most important in indicating the size of a number and approximating to the nearest 10 or 100	• read, write and order numbers up to 1000 • demonstrate that they know and can use multiplication tables • make estimates based on familiar units of measurement, checking results	• estimate distance on a map, e.g. on a 1:5000 map, 1cm = 50 metres • use a pacing scale • estimate distance in the playground - how far is the wall from the building? • measure and compare estimation of angles and bearings using half, quarter and eighth turns in a clockwise direction
LEVEL 4		
• reading, writing and ordering whole numbers • learning multiplication facts up to 10 x 10 and using them in multiplication and division problems • adding and subtracting mentally two two-digit numbers	• solve problems without the aid of a calculator, considering the reasonableness of the answer • make sensible estimates of a range of measures	• subtract start time from finish time to calculate time taken • put times into the correct order • estimate direction in degrees • estimate distance
LEVEL 5		
• understanding the notion of scale in maps and drawings	• find fractions or percentages of quantities • use units in context	• use the scale of a map to measure distance then follow the chosen route • discuss the units of measurement of scale on a map • use appropriate units for rough and fine orienteering

MATHEMATICS
AND ORIENTEERING IN THE NATIONAL CURRICULUM

SHAPE, SPACE AND MEASURES (ATTAINMENT TARGET 4)

PROGRAMME OF STUDY *Pupils should engage in activities which involve:*	STATEMENT OF ATTAINMENT *Pupils should be able to:*	EXAMPLES IN ORIENTEERING *Pupils could:*
LEVEL 1		
• sorting and classifying 2D and 3D shapes using words such as "straight", "flat", "curved", "round", "pointed", etc. • building 3D solid shapes and drawing 2D shapes and describing them • using common words, such as "on", "inside", "above", "under", "behind", "next to", to describe a position • giving and understanding instructions for movement along a route • comparing objects and ordering objects and events without measuring, using appropriate language • developing an understanding of scale including using and interpreting maps and drawings, and enlarging shapes by different scale factors	• talk about models they have made • follow or give instructions related to movement and position • compare and order objects without measuring	• describe the plan they have made from models • describe their 'treasure island' and the route they would take to find the treasure • use common words to describe the pattern and routes on a picture map
LEVEL 2		
• recognising squares, rectangles, circles, triangles, hexagons, pentagons, cubes, rectangular boxes (cuboids), cylinders and spheres and describing their properties • recognising right-angled corners in 2D and 3D shapes • recognising types of movement: straight (translation), turning (rotation) • understanding angle as a measurement of turn • understanding turning through right angles • understanding the conservation of length, capacity and 'weight'	• use mathematical terms to describe common 2D shapes and 3D objects • recognise different types of movement	• use desk top plans and picture maps • describe models for a plan using appropriate language • use language of rotation when following a route
LEVEL 3		
• sorting 2D and 3D shapes and giving reasons for each method of sorting • recognising (reflective) symmetry in a variety of shapes in two and three dimensions • using and understanding compass bearings and the terms 'clockwise' and 'anti-clockwise'	• sort shapes using mathematical criteria and give reasons • recognise reflective symmetry • use the eight points of the compass to show direction	• relate symbol shapes to the features they represent e.g. school buildings, apparatus • draw plans and matching patterns with 3D features • know where north is in the area used for orienteering
LEVEL 4		
• understanding and using language associated with angle • specifying location by means of co-ordinates in the first quadrant and by means of angle and distance	• construct 2D or 3D shapes and know associated language • specify location	• understand turning to face a new direction keeping the map set; predicting the angle of turn from the map • keep map contact whilst orienteering
LEVEL 5		
• using networks to solve problems	• use networks to solve problems	• discuss route choice problems - which is the shortest route using paths?
LEVEL 6		
• understanding and using bearings to define direction • using computers to generate and transform graphic images and to solve problems • devising of instructions for a computer to produce desired shapes and paths	• use and understand bearings to show direction	• solve a route problem using rough and fine bearings, aiming off & safety bearings

MATHEMATICS
AND ORIENTEERING IN THE NATIONAL CURRICULUM

HANDLING DATA (ATTAINMENT TARGET 5)

PROGRAMME OF STUDY *Pupils should engage in activities which involve:*	STATEMENT OF ATTAINMENT *Pupils should be able to:*	EXAMPLES IN ORIENTEERING *Pupils could:*
LEVEL 1		
• creating simple map diagrams showing relationships and interpreting them	• sort a set of objects, describing the criteria chosen	• use desk top plans
LEVEL 2		
• choosing criteria to sort and classify objects, recording results or outcomes of events • designing a data collection sheet, collecting and recording data, leading to a frequency table	• interpret relevant data which has been collected	• record results from an orienteering event • decide whether individuals should be listed separately from pairs, or boys separate from girls
LEVEL 3		
• extracting specific pieces of information from tables and lists • entering and accessing information in a simple database • entering data into a simple database; using it to find answers to simple questions	• access information in a simple database	• make a start list for a small event and discuss categories of age and sex • print out result list • find out which controls were not visited on a score course
LEVEL 4		
• inserting, interrogating and interpreting data in a computer database • specifying an issue for which data is needed • collecting, grouping, ordering discrete data using tallying methods and creating a frequency table for grouped data.	• interrogate and interpret data in a computer database • conduct a survey on an issue of their choice	• use a computer database to record results and calculate speed • devise a table for recording improvement in speed of running or orienteering • calculate average distance, points, time, speed
LEVEL 6		
• specifying an issue for which data is needed; designing and using observation sheets to collect data; collating and analysing results • designing and using a questionnaire to survey opinion • collating and analysing results	• design and use a questionnaire to survey opinion	• design a questionnaire to survey reaction to an event or participation in a trim course

PHYSICAL EDUCATION WITH OUTDOOR/ADVENTUROUS ACTIVITIES
AND ORIENTEERING IN THE NATIONAL CURRICULUM

KEY STAGE 1

PROGRAMME OF STUDY *Pupils should:*	STATEMENT OF ATTAINMENT *Pupils should be able to:*	EXAMPLES IN ORIENTEERING *Pupils could:*
GENERAL		
• be made aware of the changes that happen to their bodies during exercise	• practise and improve performance • recognise the effects of physical activity on their body • describe what they, others are doing	• run legs of a course • detect that their heart beats faster, breathing is more rapid and that they become hotter during exercise
ATHLETIC ACTIVITY		
• experience and take part in running • measure, compare and improve their own performance		• describe the route and their way of travel
OUTDOOR AND ADVENTUROUS ACTIVITIES		
• explore the potential for physical activities within one or more different environments • undertake simple orientation tasks • develop an awareness of basic safety practices • attempt challenges of a physical or problem solving nature individually and with others • develop the skills necessary for the activities undertaken		• practise orienteering games and exercises in the school hall and playground • try 'Look before you run'. Reading a map well means you can find your way and not get lost so easily. • plan courses in the school grounds with and for others

21

PHYSICAL EDUCATION WITH OUTDOOR/ADVENTUROUS ACTIVITIES AND ORIENTEERING IN THE NATIONAL CURRICULUM

KEY STAGE 2

PROGRAMME OF STUDY Pupils should:	STATEMENT OF ATTAINMENT Pupils should be able to:	EXAMPLES IN ORIENTEERING Pupils could:
GENERAL		
• be enabled to respond quickly to changing environments or adjust to other people's actions	• perform effectively in activities requiring quick decision-making	• practise quick decision-making during competitive orienteering games - where am I? - which way do I go? - what do I follow?
• be given opportunities to work alone to ensure the development of their own personal skills	• respond safely, alone and with others, to challenging tasks taking account of levels of skill and understanding	• use star exercises to encourage working alone in an unfamiliar area. Every child always has his/her own map
• be taught to help themselves to improve by making simple comments and judgements on their own performance and that of others	• evaluate how well they and others perform and behave against criteria suggested by the teacher, and suggest ways of improving performance	• find control points in a limited time - score orienteering
		• practise, listen, watch, help others in order to improve. Analyse perform-ance to show areas of skill which need improvement and keep training diaries
		• go running and orienteering whenever possible. Recognise improvement of skills through practice
• be taught to understand the value of and demonstrate sustained activity over appropriate periods of time	• sustain energetic activity over appropriate periods of time in a range of physical activities and understand the effects of exercise on the body	• use orienteering to observe changes in pulse rate, breathing, body temperature. Heart muscles will adapt to exercise and become more efficient. Fitness is increased
• be taught to understand the immediate and short term effects of exercise on the body		• learn to wear appropriate clothing, and not to eat or drink before running. Gen-tle use of muscles and joints before any fast activity - 'warm up the engine before driving it fast'. Keep warm after activity. Shower. Change clothes
• be taught to understand and demon-strate how to prepare for particular activities and how to recover afterwards		
ATHLETIC ACTIVITY		
• practise and develop basic actions in running		• run in different terrains
• experience competitions including those they make up themselves		• experience cross country, score, line and relay events
OUTDOOR AND ADVENTUROUS ACTIVITIES		
• learn the principles of safety in the outdoors and develop the ability to assess and respond to challenges in a variety of contexts and conditions		• learn about safety bearings, emergency whistle signal, what to do when lost, re-porting to the finish, appropriate clothing
• experience outdoor and adventurous activities in different environments (such as school grounds, parks or woodland) that involve planning, navigation, working in small groups, recording and evaluating		• learn responsible behaviour - care of the environment, care of each other. Fair play - no cheating. Care of activity - do not move control markers
		• go orienteering in school grounds, parks or woodland, organise an orienteering event, analyse individual performance
• be taught the skills necessary for the activity undertaken with due regard for safety including the correct use of appropriate equipment		• learn that skilful use of map and com-pass in orienteering gives knowledge and experience needed to navigate anywhere in safety

GEOGRAPHY
AND ORIENTEERING IN THE NATIONAL CURRICULUM

GEOGRAPHICAL SKILLS

Enquiry should form an important part of pupils' work in geography in Key Stage 1. Work should be linked to pupils' own interests, experience and capabilities and should lead to investigations based on fieldwork and classroom activities. Much of pupils' learning in Key Stage 1 should be based on direct experience, practical activities and exploration of the local area

PROGRAMME OF STUDY Pupils should engage in activities which:	STATEMENT OF ATTAINMENT Pupils should be able to:	EXAMPLES IN ORIENTEERING Pupils could:
LEVEL 1		
• follow directions, including the terms forwards, backwards, up and down, left, right, north, south, east, west	• follow directions • make observations about physical and human features of places	• follow routes using desk top and classroom plans
LEVEL 2		
• extract information from, and add it to, pictorial maps • draw around objects to make a plan, e.g. mathematical shapes, etc. • make representations of actual or imaginary places, e.g. their own bedroom, a treasure island • follow a route on a map, e.g. a map of the local area of the school • use pictures and photographs to identify features, e.g. homes, railways, rivers, hills and to find out about places	• use geographical vocabulary to talk about places including those beyond their own locality • make a representation of a real or an imaginary place • follow a route using a plan • identify familiar features on photographs and pictures	• make picture maps and plans • make their own 'treasure island' map • follow routes on their treasure island map • use air photographs to identify map features • organise a classroom score event
LEVEL 3		
• use the eight points of the compass • make a map of a short route, showing main features in the correct order, *e.g. from home to school* • locate their own position and identify features using a large scale map • identify features on oblique air photos	• use a large scale map to locate their own position and features outside the classroom • make a map of a short route, showing features in the correct order • identify features on air photographs	• use orienteering as a medium to show the importance of the compass directions • use the map of the school or local park for orienteering exercises
LEVEL 4		
• use pictures and photographs to identify features, *e.g. homes, railways, rivers, hills* and to find out about places; describe what they see using geographical terms • interpret symbols, measure direction and distance, follow routes and describe the location of places using maps • make representations of real or imaginary places; make and use maps of routes, and sketch maps of small areas showing the main features and using symbols with keys • use the eight points of the compass • determine the straight line distance between two points on a map	• measure the straight line distance between two points on a plan draw a sketch map using symbols and a key	• measure distance taken on various routes • use a compass to reset the map • draw maps of apparatus inside as part of the school grounds
LEVEL 5		
• locate their position and identify features outside the classroom using a large scale map • identify features on vertical air photographs, e.g. railway lines, rivers and roads and match them to a map • use maps to find out where features are located and activities take place	• interpret relief maps	• start learning about contours
LEVEL 6		
	• use map and compass to follow a route	• practise rough/fine bearings, aiming off • make a map
LEVEL 7		
	• examine the interaction of human and physical processes in shaping environments	• study the legend of a local map to distinguish between natural and man-made features

GEOGRAPHY
AND ORIENTEERING IN THE NATIONAL CURRICULUM

PLACES

PROGRAMME OF STUDY *Pupils should be taught:*	STATEMENT OF ATTAINMENT *Pupils should be able to:*	EXAMPLES IN ORIENTEERING *Pupils could:*
	LEVEL 1	
Pupils should develop their awareness of localities in and beyond their own neighbourhood. Where possible such teaching should build on pupils' experience from visits, but should also use secondary sources, for example photographs, objects, stories, videos and accounts by teachers and other adults	• name familiar features of the local area	• become familiar with the school map • look at maps of the local area
	LEVEL 2	
A locality should be a small area with distinctive features, e.g. the immediate vicinity of the school or of the pupil's home	• to appreciate attractive and unattractive features of a local environment • differentiate between physical and human features of different environments	
	LEVEL 3	
• to identify and describe landscape features in the local area, e.g. building, park, river, hill, valley, lake with which they are familiar	• use correct geographical vocabulary to identify types of landscape features and activities with which they are familiar in the local area • use a variety of map scales	• use appropriate vocabulary to identify features on areas to be visited for orienteering • compare orienteering map scales

GEOGRAPHY
AND ORIENTEERING IN THE NATIONAL CURRICULUM

THEMATIC STUDIES

PROGRAMME OF STUDY	STATEMENT OF ATTAINMENT *Pupils should be able to:*	EXAMPLES IN ORIENTEERING *Pupils could:*
	LEVEL 2	
• to identify activities which have changed the environment and consider ways in which they can improve their own environment	• describe ways in which people have changed the environment	• discuss if the school playground is a good environment for orienteering, a woodland sport? Could it be improved? Are we spoiling any part of the playground by orienteering?
	LEVEL 3	
• about activities intended to improve the local environment or a place they have visited	• describe effects on different environments of extracting natural resources	• describe some of the effects on landscape and wildlife caused by clearing woodland
	LEVEL 4	
• ways in which people look after and improve the environment; some of the ways in which damaged environments can be restored and damage prevented; and to consider whether some types of environment need special protection	• discuss whether some types of environment need special protection • describe ways in which damaged landscapes can be restored • study the effect of weather, water and human settlement on particular environments	• discuss the problems of protecting special habitats of plants or wildlife where orienteers might run, such as wet marshland or rare woodland. Consider the positioning of control points

4 Lesson plans

INDEX OF LESSON PLANS

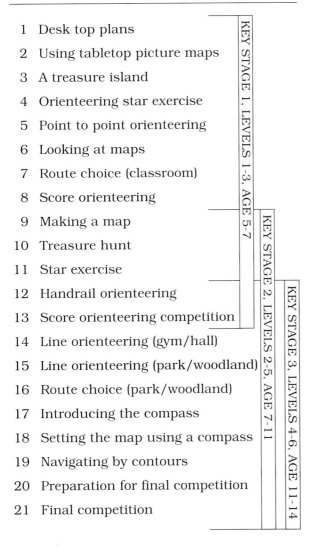
INTRODUCTION

The following lessons enable the teacher to deliver attainment targets of the National Curriculum.

They also give a grounding in basic skills. Like most sports, orienteering has basic skills. These are:

> Knowledge of map symbols
> Orientating the map
> Following handrails
> Relocation
> Route choice
> Use of compass
> Simplifying navigational problems

The fundamental skill in orienteering is orientating the map. The key to moving with a map is recognising the pattern of objects on the ground as the same as the pattern on the map and ALWAYS holding the map so that you are looking along the route to be followed. Orientating the map is a thread which runs through all the lesson plans that follow.

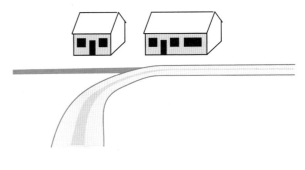

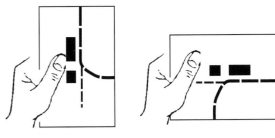

Orientate the map to correspond with the terrain. The map can also be orientated with the help of a compass (see lesson 17).

DESK TOP PLANS:
SHAPES AND RELATIONSHIPS
IN THE CLASSROOM

NATIONAL CURRICULUM

Geography   Key Stage 1
Mathematics Key Stage 1

OBJECTIVES
- *To introduce the concept that maps and plans are a pattern of shapes*
- *To draw around objects to make a plan*
- *The use of words to describe position*
- *To develop understanding of the following terms:*
  SHAPES, PATTERN, PLAN, MATCHING

EQUIPMENT

Models of houses, trees and fences
Paper, pencils, coloured pencils/crayons
Coloured paper

Teacher preparation

Collect landscape models or objects with clear and contrasting shapes

Lesson

1. Place three objects on a sheet of paper in a very simple **pattern**. Draw round each piece then remove the objects to show the outline **shapes**. Discuss which shape **matches** which object and what shape each one is. A **plan** has been produced of the model.

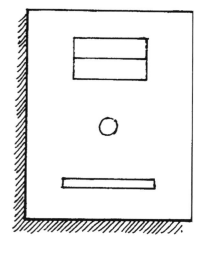

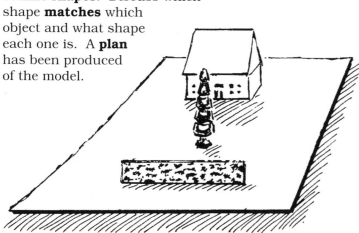

2. Place the objects in a different relationship. Draw the correct shapes on a piece of paper next to the model. Involve the children in deciding what shape to draw and where it should go. If the map is to be correct the drawing must match the model.

3. Give out paper and ask the children to draw the correct shapes in the right pattern. Place the objects on a central table, or use sets of objects with smaller groups of children.

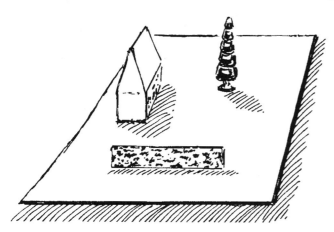

4. *Find the treasure*

Gather the class round the central table keeping the same pattern of objects, with each child having his/her own plan.

The children close their eyes while the teacher puts a cross or 'T' (for treasure) on the paper underneath part of one of the objects e.g. under the corner of a house. The teacher shows the class where the treasure is on the plan by marking on a red circle, then, pointing to the model, asks "Where is the treasure hidden?"

This should be repeated a few times. The **plan** must **match** the model if the treasure is to be found easily.

Next, let the children see where the treasure is to be hidden and ask them to mark on their plans where the treasure is to be found. This again can be repeated.

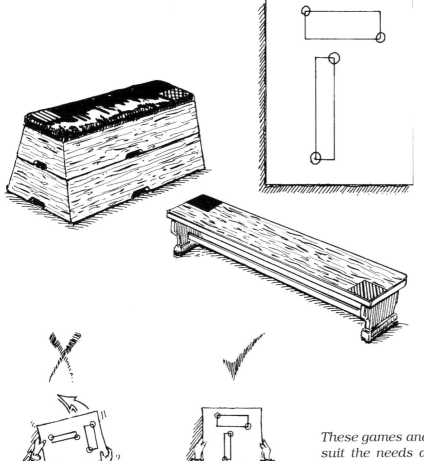

5. In a larger area, lay out two pieces of apparatus or furniture in a clear pattern. The children draw shapes to match. Some children may find this difficult.

Place a piece of coloured paper with 2-3 matching coloured crayons on one corner of each end of each piece of apparatus. Each child draws a circle on his/her plan to indicate where the paper is. The children must **match** their plans to the apparatus (i.e. hold them the right way round) all the time.

6. Demonstrate that if you turn your plan a different way round the shapes do not match the apparatus. When the children have tried this for themselves, ask them to colour in the circles.

These games and exercises can be adapted to suit the needs and ability of your particular group of children. For example, the children of a class which understands these ideas quickly could practise walking towards a piece of apparatus from different parts of the area, keeping the plan set as they move.

<table>
<tr><td>

LESSON

2

</td><td>

USING TABLETOP PICTURE MAPS
IN THE CLASSROOM

</td><td>

NATIONAL CURRICULUM

Geography   Key Stage 1
Mathematics Key Stage 1

</td></tr>
</table>

OBJECTIVES
* *To reinforce the concept that a map is like a picture*
* *To see how a map can be used to show, and help you follow, a route*
* *To locate positions on a map*
* *To follow directions*
* *To develop understanding of the following terms:*
  PICTURE MAP, SET, ROUTE, SYMBOLS, PLAN, DIRECTIONS

EQUIPMENT
Tabletop picture maps
Coloured pencils
Model houses and trees and a model car
String
Boards to lean on

Teacher preparation

Draw a simple picture map and a plan of a table top model or copy the ones shown on the next page.

Lesson

1. Set up the model to match the map. Give each child a copy of the picture map. The children should stand or sit round 3 sides of the model so that they can relate their picture maps to the model. Ask them to **set** their maps and identify each of the houses and trees.

2. Introduce the model car, which is going on a tour, visiting each of the houses. As the car is directed along its **route** the children follow where it goes on their picture maps, continually locating its position. Use the terms 'left' and 'right'.

3. Choose a new starting point. The children now draw in the route the car takes as it goes from house to house. A piece of string showing the route on the model will help them to draw the correct line. Arrows on the line will show the direction the car is going.

4. Give each child a **plan** of the model. Compare and match the picture map and the plan with each other and with the model. Identify the **symbols** showing trees and houses. **Set** the plan. Locate the start point of the route shown by the string and already drawn on the picture maps.

Draw the route on to the plan by looking at the line of the string. Compare it with the line on the picture map.

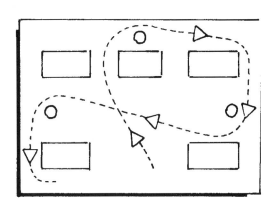

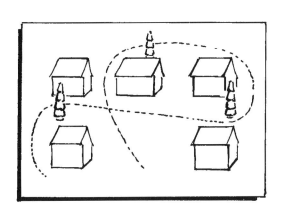

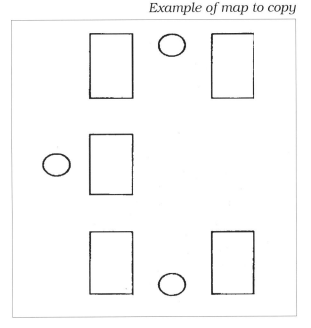

Summary

Maps are made up of **symbols**. Symbols are map language. The symbols can be read and seen as pictures of the features they represent. A map can be used to plan and follow a **route.**

Follow up

Children can make their own models and then make picture maps or plans of them. Plot in routes using string, and then transfer them onto the map.

The same lesson can be used to introduce the cardinal compass points, along with a globe and maps of the world. Use the compass to establish north. Place the model orientated to north. Label the model and the plans, marking north, south, east and west. Describe the location and direction of the features. Describe the routes according to directions taken.

Example of map to copy

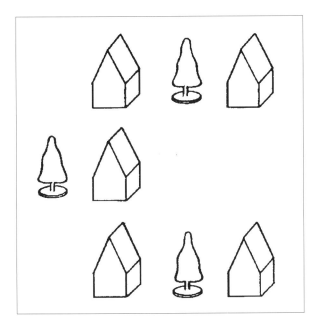

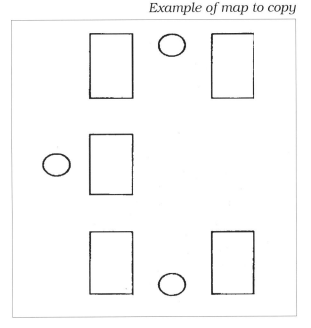

LESSON **3**	**A TREASURE ISLAND** IN THE CLASSROOM OR HALL

A TREASURE ISLAND

IN THE CLASSROOM OR HALL

OBJECTIVES
- *To establish the meaning of the word "set" and follow up the use of shapes and symbols*
- *To extract information and add it to pictorial maps*
- *To make representation of imaginary places*
- *To follow a route and locate position*
- *To give instructions for movement along a route*
- *To develop understanding of the following terms:*
  MAP, SET, ROUTE

NATIONAL CURRICULUM

Geography   Key Stage 1
Mathematics Key Stage 1

EQUIPMENT
Treasure island features, e.g. lake (water basin), river (blue rope or cord), house (box), trees (skittles or cones), field (outline with canes or rope), tracks (chalked lines) + paper, clipboards, crayons (blue, green, black, brown, red),

Teacher preparation

Collect equipment. Decide which area to use: younger children need to be able to overlook the whole area; older ones can use a larger area with bigger features. Read a story about an island.

Lesson

1. Give out paper, boards, crayons. Seat the children round the area to be used for the island.

2. Using chalk or rope, mark out the coastline of the island in a simple shape. As you add features on the island, the children draw them on their own paper. A mixture of pictures and symbols is quite acceptable for this map.

3. Place large features first: the lake (basin of water) and the river (blue cord) leading to it;

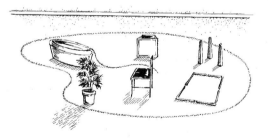

the box as the house; the cones (or pot plants) can represent trees; a chair can be a lookout tower. A field can be used to fill in the gaps.

4. Story line

Following a shipwreck a box of treasure is buried. Before being rescued the mariners make a **map** of the island so that the treasure can be found later. The children are the shipwrecked mariners.

Ask the children where they want to bury their treasure. Mark the place with a "T".

Now years later you return to dig up your treasure and land on the island at the point where you are sitting. Mark it on your map with an arrow.

t = treasure

5. "Which **route** will you take to get to the treasure?" The teacher demonstrates. Plan the route looking at the model, then trace it on the map with a finger. The map must be kept **set** to follow the route. A few children can talk through the route which they would follow, identifying the features they will pass by pointing at the model or the map.

6. If the island is big enough, the children can then try to follow the **route**, walking from one feature to the next until the treasure is reached.

7. Add north, south, east and west to the model and maps, then use those terms to describe positions and routes, e.g. Kay sits between the south and east ends of the island, the house is in the north.

Follow up

Talk about islands. Collect information about islands such as Australia, Britain or Iceland. Make maps of other areas or models. **This is an ideal starting point for cross-curricular work**. Children can make their own imaginary island with features and treasure sites. Use this to talk about the island and make problems for friends to solve.

LESSON 4

ORIENTEERING STAR EXERCISE
IN THE PLAYGROUND OR SCHOOL FIELD

OBJECTIVES
- *To introduce orienteering*
- *To find features (controls) which are out of sight using a large scale map*
- *To locate positions*
- *To practise and improve performance*
- *To undertake simple orientation activity*
- *Decision making*
- *To develop understanding of the following terms:*
  ORIENTEERING, SET, CONTROL FLAGS

NATIONAL CURRICULUM

Geography   Key Stage 1
Mathematics Key Stage 1
Phys. Ed.   Key Stage 1

EQUIPMENT
Boards, size approximately 20 x 20 cm
Maps of the school and playground
8-10 mini-controls or coloured tapes
8-10 coloured wax crayons with string
Enlarged copy of map (approx A3) on board

Teacher preparation

Plan 8-10 control sites, some within sight and others just out of sight of the base/start. Mark the controls on all the maps, including the enlarged version, with red circles. (Use a circle template.) Number each circle. Tape the maps to the boards. Hang the control markers and crayons at the controls. Use the same start/base as for lesson 3.

Lesson

1. Give each child a map on a board. Go outside to the base shown as the triangle on the map. Set the map and discuss the features and symbols.

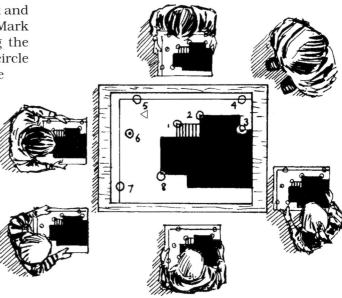

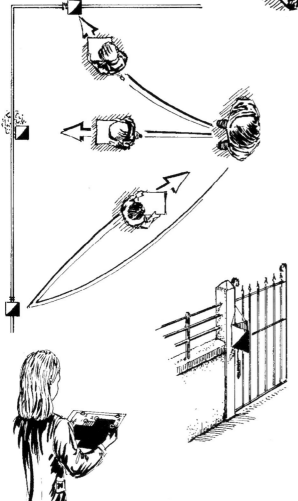

The large A3 size map is useful for demonstrating how to set the map.

Identify (point out) a control. Set the map. Teacher and children run to the control. Repeat a few times, checking that everyone can set the map. Use a distinctive wall, hedge or road to help match the map to the ground. Point out the crayon hanging from the control.

2. Star exercise: each child is given one control to find. The child has to go to the control, colour in the right circle on the map with the crayon hanging there then return to base to join the queue ready for the teacher to identify the next control to visit.

Before running off the child should point out to the teacher the control flag he/she is going to, or, if it is out of sight, describe where it is.

Continue until most of the children have all the circles coloured in. Check that the colours are correct.

Further work

Some children could now go round the controls in a given order, marking control card boxes with the correct colour.

LESSON 5

POINT TO POINT ORIENTEERING
IN THE PLAYGROUND OR SCHOOL FIELD

OBJECTIVES
- *To remind the children that they should see the map as a picture*
- *To teach change of direction on the orientated map*
- *To practise orientation*
- *To practise locating their own position in relation to the landscape*
- *To recognise angles as a measurement of turn*
- *To develop understanding of the following terms:*
  KEEP THE MAP SET, ORIENTEERING, ROUTE, ORIENTATION

NATIONAL CURRICULUM

Geography   Key Stage 1
Mathematics Key Stage 1
Phys. Ed.   Key Stage 1

EQUIPMENT
6-8 mini-control markers (or coloured tapes)
with wax crayons or clip punches attached
A large (A3) map of the school and grounds
Small (A5) maps of the school and grounds
with control boxes down one edge

Teacher preparation

Plan 6-8 control sites. They should be mostly different from those used for lesson 4. Mark all the control sites on all the children's maps with red circles. Mark the start/finish with a triangle. Highlight a strip down one edge of the map with a bright colour. This need not necessarily be North, rather a hedge or wall which will act as the main reference line for setting the map. Hang the controls and crayons (or clip punches).

Lesson

1. In the classroom: Evaluate the group's understanding of the playground map and the symbols used. Look at the large map of the school and ask individual children to identify specific features e.g "Which entrance do you use to come into the school?"; "Which area is used for play at break time?" Ask them to close their eyes and imagine what each feature looks like: "Make a picture of it in your head". This is how they should 'read the map'.

2. Outside: Start at the triangle. Set the map using the coloured edge to help. Lay the map on the ground in front of you, still set.

   On the map, find the control with number "1" beside it. This is the first control. Walk around the set map until you are looking in the direction of the control as viewed from the start. Pick up the map. The map is set. You are facing along the route you want to follow. DEMONSTRATE CLEARLY.

3. All go to control 1. Do not use the crayon (or clip punches).

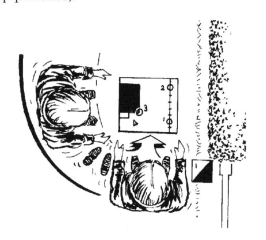

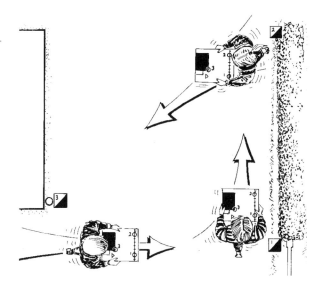

At each control follow this procedure:
- Set the map (on the ground, if this helps)
- Find the next control on the map. What is it?
- Walk around the map until you are facing the right way.
- Look. Can you see the marker? If not, plan your route.

(To promote individual decision making:)
- Make up your own mind about which way you should face.

Send the children round the course individually to practise this on their own. This time they should mark the control boxes with the coloured crayons (or clip with the punches). Start each child off as soon as the last has left the first control.

4. After each child has visited all the controls in the right order, send him/her round again. This time the circles on the map can be coloured in. The children needing extra help will have been identified by this time, and can be given more attention.

Further work

Draw symbols and write the name beside each.
Show a video about orienteering.
Find out when there will be a local event (see p.64 for addresses for information) and send information home to the parents to encourage the family to take part.

LESSON 6	LOOKING AT MAPS IN THE CLASSROOM AND PLAYGROUND

NATIONAL CURRICULUM

Geography   Key Stage 1
Phys. Ed.   Key Stage 1

OBJECTIVES
• To use pictures and photographs to identify features
• To explore the potential for physical activity within the immediate environment
• To develop understanding of the following terms:
   PLANS, MAPS, SYMBOLS, ROUTE, ORIENTEERING, CONTROL, RUNNING

EQUIPMENT
Local map including school + photocopies
10-15 mini/micro orienteering controls
Comprehensive selection of maps
Street plans, globe, world map, atlas
Adhesive, string, paper, pencils

Teacher preparation
Display maps.
Set out 10-15 controls.

General introduction
Children should be encouraged to bring in a wide variety of maps and a colourful wall dis-play should be made. Try to use a collection of orienteering maps for one corner of the display - contact your local orienteering club for help.

Discuss the different map sizes, colours, why and how maps are used. Remind them about the idea of the map being an aerial or bird's-eye view of the ground. Each object or feature on the ground has a relationship with every other feature. This is reflected by the map. The map should be seen as a picture with all the features seen in the same relationship or pattern as those on the ground. The map can be pictured as a 3-dimensional model or miniature of the landscape, just like their tabletop maps.

Discuss the use of symbols on maps.

Use a road map to set tasks, e.g. finding the shortest route between towns.

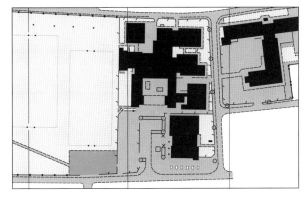

Introduce the orienteering map. Explain the accuracy, detail and why it has been drawn, for a sport that involves running and map reading, called orienteering. Show the orienteering controls already used in the playground.

Practical
Playground game: the teacher puts out 10-15 controls, using adhesive or string, on prominent features, e.g. gate, football post, steps, etc. They should be between knee and head height. No map is used.

The children find as many controls as they can in a given time, e.g. 10 minutes. They carry paper and pencil and make a list of the code letters on each control.

If you have a map of the school, help the children to identify where the controls were found. Back in the classroom the letters could be used to make up words.

Physical Education
Use this opportunity to observe the changes to their bodies during 10 minutes running, e.g. becoming hot, breathing faster, sweating, heart beating faster, feeling tired, sore, thirsty.

LESSON 7

ROUTE CHOICE
IN THE CLASSROOM AND PLAYGROUND

NATIONAL CURRICULUM

Geography   Key Stage 1 & 2
Phys. Ed.   Key Stage 1 & 2
Mathematics Key Stage 1

OBJECTIVES
* *To build children's awareness and appreciation of maps through using them*
* *Decision making*
* *To develop understanding of the following terms:*
  ROUTE CHOICE, ORIENTEERING COURSE

EQUIPMENT
Local street map including school (one/child)
Playground maps premarked with lesson 6
   control sites
10-15 mini controls
Coloured cotton, chalk or crayons

Teacher preparation
Obtain maps. Place controls.

Classroom activity
Distribute local street maps and ask the children to find the school, their own street, the nearest train/bus station, a church, a supermarket, etc. Have children draw in features not already included, make a key if necessary and colour in the map if suitable.

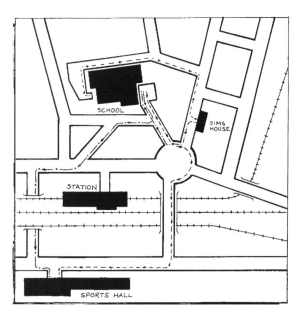

Tasks: children locate their homes and work out the routes they take to school, and other journeys.

Emphasise route choice. Children work out two or more routes between two places. Routes can be shown in different colours using chalk, crayons or cotton. The routes could be discussed using an OHP.
   Explain that in the sport of orienteering, runners often have a choice of route when they have to find control points on their course.

Practical
Distribute the playground maps with the controls marked on from lesson 6.
   In the classroom, the children decide as individuals or as pairs in which order they will find all the controls. They then go and find them, copying each code letter onto their map.

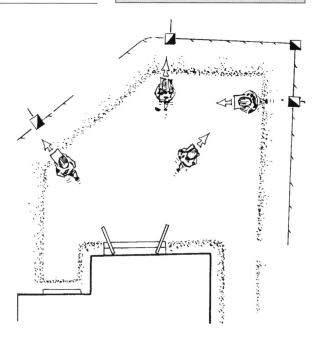

The children then repeat this exercise, but plan and visit the controls in a completely different order. Remind them to always set the map before going to next control.

This exercise emphasises that the problems presented can be solved in different ways. On the second attempt, running can be encouraged.

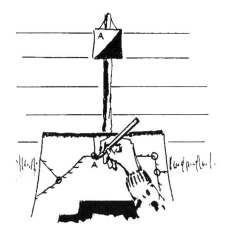

<table>
<tr><td>
LESSON

8
</td><td>

SCORE ORIENTEERING
IN THE CLASSROOM AND GYMNASIUM/HALL
</td></tr>
</table>

NATIONAL CURRICULUM

Geography	Key Stage 1 & 2
Phys. Ed.	Key Stage 1 & 2
Mathematics	Key Stage 1

OBJECTIVES
- *To introduce score orienteering using a classroom map*
- *To locate features using a large scale map*
- *To use north to set the map*
- *To introduce rules in competition*
- *To develop understanding of the following terms:*
  POINT TO POINT, SCORE ORIENTEERING

EQUIPMENT
2 sets of matching cards (with different symbols drawn on)
Classroom maps
Mini controls
Adhesive (blu-tak), paper and pencils

Teacher preparation

Copy a good map of the classroom. Make one set of 10 cards with different symbols on each card and number them. Make an identical set of 10 cards but put letters on them.

Classroom activity

Introduce the map of the classroom made by the teacher. Give one copy to each child.

Pupils mark their places with triangles. In orienteering the start is always shown with a triangle.

Mark the north edge of the map with a red crayon.

Place 10 lettered micro markers each on a different distinctive feature.

As each one is placed, the children mark the position on their maps with a clear circle in red and a number *beside* it, not in the middle. Do not allow the children to colour in the circles or triangle, otherwise the map detail will be hidden.

Teach map setting - make sure everything matches and *map north* is always to the *north end* of the classroom. Is it easier to set the map if you know where north is?

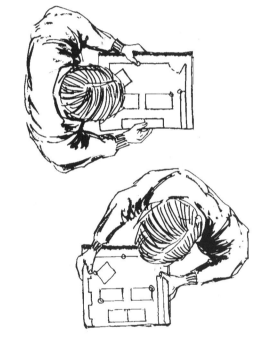

Ask the children to find each control, in any order, and mark the letter found on the control beside the appropriate circle on their map. They return to their seats when finished.

Give 10 points for each control (everyone should get 100 points). During the exercise check that the children:
(i) do not just spot the controls by looking around but read the map to decide where they are, and
(ii) keep the map set.

Explain *score orienteering* and show how it differs from *point to point orienteering* - see lesson 5.

LESSON 9	MAKING A MAP IN THE GYMNASIUM/HALL	NATIONAL CURRICULUM **Geography** Key Stage 1 & 2 **Phys. Ed.** Key Stage 1 & 2 **Mathematics** Key Stage 1

OBJECTIVES
- *To draw and then use a map of the gymnasium/hall*
- *To make a map with symbols and a key*
- *To introduce scale*
- *To develop understanding of the following terms:*
  MAPPING, SCALE, 'FOREST', PLOTTING

EQUIPMENT
Gymnastic apparatus, e.g. mats, benches,
  hoops, boxes, etc.
Rulers
Red marker
Paper and pencils

Teacher preparation

Plan the layout of the apparatus. Draw a sample map.

Practical (in the gym or a defined playground area such as a netball court)
Each child has an A4 sheet of white paper, pencil and ruler. Children with learning difficulties should be given a copy of the map almost complete.

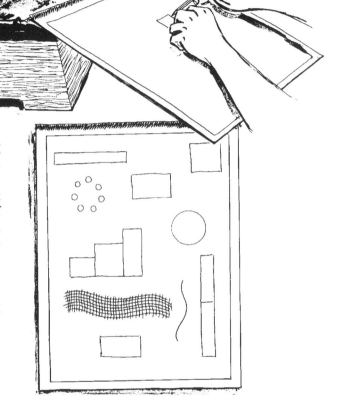

Ask the children to imagine they are looking down on the area from the ceiling. They are going to produce a map of the area.

Suggest the outline is drawn first. Check when this has been completed to see that all of the A4 sheet has been used. If some children have drawn the four walls too small, use the different sizes of outline to introduce the concept of scale. Mark the north edge with red.

Create a 'forest' in the gym/hall by laying out a variety of gymnastic equipment, e.g. mats, benches, hoops, table, badminton net (descibed as a 'river'). Make sure the initial 'forest' is simple and keep the benches, boxes and mats parallel to the walls.

Teach the children to plot the features onto their maps starting with the most obvious large feature in the centre. Then use this as the basis for fixing the next feature.

Using the apparatus laid out to make a 'forest', take the children for a 'forest' walk. Suggest they keep the map set as they walk through the 'forest'. The teacher should demonstrate setting the map each time direction is changed. The children can then work in pairs, taking it in turn to lead, running once they can keep the map set.

Aim for 6-7 minutes running.

The map can be taken back to the classroom, redrawn and coloured with a key added.

TREASURE HUNT
IN THE PLAYGROUND OR SCHOOL FIELD

NATIONAL CURRICULUM

Geography   Key Stage 1 & 2
Mathematics Key Stage 1

OBJECTIVES
- *To construct and use small maps of parts of the playground or field*
- *To establish the concept of pattern and relationship of one feature with another*
- *To develop understanding of the following terms:*
  TREASURE HUNT, MAP MAKING, DIRECTION

EQUIPMENT
'Treasure', e.g. class first names on pieces of card
'Big treasure', e.g. packet of sweets
Clipboards
Paper, pencils and crayons

Teacher preparation

Make name cards, place them in the playground. Make a sample map of the area to be used. Make cards for the location of the 'big treasure'.

Practical

Take the children outside to a suitable part of the playground or school field, containing very little other than a couple of buildings.

The children make a very simple map of this area. The emphasis, as in earlier mapping lessons, is on placing features in the right relationship to each other.

North, south, east and west (N, S, E, W) can be marked on the maps and used in discussion, e.g. the playing field is on the north side of the map.

When the map is completed, play 'treasure hunt'.

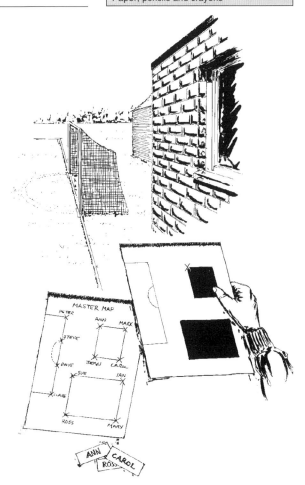

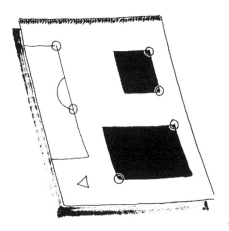

Treasure hunt

The teacher has placed a number of pieces of 'treasure' at distinct points within the area of the map. The children locate one piece of treasure at a time. The teacher marks an X on each child's map which he/she uses to find the right treasure. They leave the treasure in place and report back what they have found.

The children change maps and find new treasure using a map with a different X on it.

Collect in these treasures.

The teacher then puts out the 'big treasure' location cards in the same area.

The children visit the control sites in any order, write down all the words, then work out the message which indicates the location of the big treasure, e.g. a packet of sweets. They could work in pairs for this game.

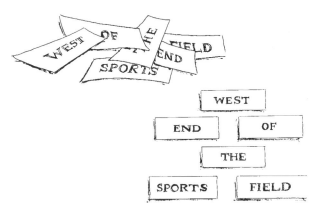

	WEST	
END		OF
	THE	
SPORTS		FIELD

LESSON 11	**STAR EXERCISE** IN THE PLAYGROUND OR SCHOOL FIELD

OBJECTIVES
- *To introduce the new playground map*
- *To reinforce setting the map, orientation activity*
- *To help children maintain contact with the map as they move about*
- *To improve performance through practice*
- *To develop understanding of the following terms:*
  MAP CONTACT, SETTING THE MAP, STAR EXERCISE

NATIONAL CURRICULUM

Geography   Key Stage 1 & 2
Phys. Ed.   Key Stage 1 & 2
Mathematics Key Stage 1

EQUIPMENT
Mini markers with numbers and code letters
Red crayons/pens
Playground maps
Pencils

Teacher preparation

This lesson is similar to lesson 4, using a map of a larger area, with controls further away from the base. Hang 8-10 mini markers on definite features in the play-ground or school field. Make a master map and plan a route to include all the controls.

Practical

Using the playground map, take the class for a map walk. Each child must have his/her own map. Insist that the map is correctly set and that the children are able to point to their position on the map whenever they stop.
NB Orienteers fold their maps and hold them with the thumb beside their last known position. This is part of keeping **map contact**.

During the walk, point out features and ask the children questions about map/terrain details. Ensure this is done slowly so that all children are always aware of their position on the map. The walk should lead past the mini markers which have been hung on definite features which are also on the map, e.g. 'fence corner' not just 'fence'.

At each marker the children draw a circle on their maps in the correct place. Check that they get this exactly right. Number the circles.

Star exercise

This is one of the best orienteering exercises for teaching skills to mixed ability groups. Individuals can work at their own pace and the teacher is in contact with the whole class. Each child will return to the base (triangle) after finding each control.

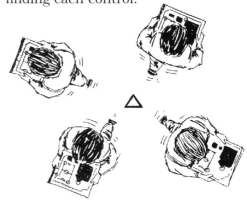

Number the children to indicate which control each one is to find first, e.g. number 6 goes to control 6 first.

Emphasise to the children that they must return after each control, remembering the code letter. The teacher checks that they have memorised the correct letter.

Each time he/she returns to base, the map must be set with the child facing the right direction before going to the next control. The teacher can give help to those who need it.

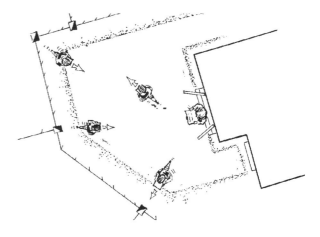

LESSON 12	HANDRAIL ORIENTEERING

HANDRAIL ORIENTEERING
IN SCHOOL FIELD, PARK OR WOODLAND

OBJECTIVES
- *To show how line features can be used to make safe, fast route choices thereby simplifying navigation.*
- *To encourage map observation and decision making.*
- *To encourage compass work and distance judgement as back-up skills to map reading.*
- *To encourage discussion and evaluation afterwards on the best routes.*

NATIONAL CURRICULUM

Phys. Ed.	Key Stages 2 & 3
Geography	Key Stages 2 & 3
Mathematics	Key Stages 2 & 3
English	Key Stages 2 & 3

EQUIPMENT
Maps and control markers
Pencils or punches as available
Control cards
Red biros
Compasses

Teacher preparation

Plan a course of 1-2 kilometres with controls on or beside clear line features (e.g. path/stream crossing) and route choices between them which encourage 'handrail' navigation.

Pre-mark the course with straight lines between controls so that pupils choose their own line features to follow - or prepare master maps for the children to copy down the course themselves onto their own map. The use of covered maps which can be marked and wiped off will economise on map stocks - or sets of maps made up for each lesson.

Emphasise to the children that:
- They have to form their own plan of action in navigating from one control to another.
- Using 'line features' as 'handrails' in a 'roundabout' way is safer than always going straight or trying to cut corners.
- Distance judgement is a very useful 'back-up' technique to ensure the path chosen is going in the right direction and, if the control is just off the path, that you have come the right distance to turn off and 'hit' it.
- Handrail navigation means that if you do get lost you can retrace your steps more easily to find where you are again.

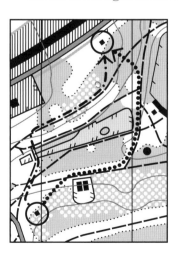

- Running on a path can be much quicker than walking across rough ground or through thick trees and that climbing hills is often slower than taking tracks round them.
- The 'tortoise' who stays with line features and does not make mistakes will beat the 'hare' who runs haphazardly.

Practical exercise

The pupils are set off at 1-2 minute intervals singly or in pairs and do the course as quickly as possible choosing their own routes and marking them on their maps afterwards. They punch or write down a marker code onto a card at each control point as proof of visit.

The teacher can time or not depending on the experience of the group.

Adaptations and further work

- For large groups of children, two or three or more handrail loops can be planned to stop 'following'. See alternative lesson 21, page 51.
- Pupils can mark on selected routes before they start if they are relatively inexperienced.
- Make a set of route choice cards - pieces of map with 2 controls showing a line feature route choice leg. Use these to discuss route choice decisions. This is useful both <u>before</u> and after the lesson.

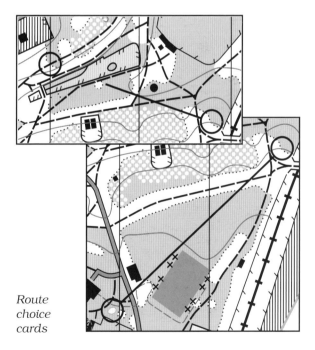

Route choice cards

Evaluation

Pupils should be encouraged to draw their own routes on the map or a photocopy after the event, to exchange maps with a partner and to compare use of line features. Could they have used better handrails? Why did they make mistakes? How did they find themselves again and how quickly? How could they have completed the course faster?

LESSON 13	**SCORE ORIENTEERING COMPETITION** IN THE PLAYGROUND, SCHOOL FIELD OR LOCAL PARK

NATIONAL CURRICULUM	
Geography	Key Stages 1, 2 & 3
Phys. Ed.	Key Stages 1, 2 & 3
Mathematics	Key Stages 1, 2 & 3
+ Social	

OBJECTIVES
- *To complete the block of work with a class competition*
- *To promote individual decision making*
- *To develop understanding of the following terms:*
  MASTER MAP, SCORE EVENT, THINKING SEQUENCE

EQUIPMENT
10-15 mini markers with numbers and code letters
Master maps
Clock
Start banner

Teacher preparation

Set up a score event, hanging 10-15 mini markers on distinctive features marked on the map. Each marker should be visible (not hidden) so that the children can find them by reading the map. Draw up 4-5 master maps.

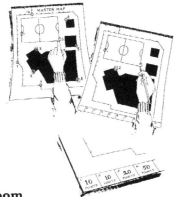

Classroom

Children prepare or the score event by:
- drawing boxes in spaces round the outside edge (not the back) of the front of the map, so that the control codes can be copied when each control is found.
- copying the controls from a master map on to their own maps.

Teach them to point with a finger to a control on the master map when copying that control.

Practical

Set a time limit for the children to complete the course, e.g. 15 minutes. Explain that the purpose of the competition is to visit as many controls as possible within the time.

The controls can be visited in any order. Each control is worth a number of points (10 is the simplest) so they are trying to achieve as high a score as possible within the time. If they take longer they will have points deducted for each minute late. A very lenient penalty would be minus 5 per minute as it would probably take less than a minute to return from the farthest point of the playground.

Remind the children of the skills needed to find controls successfully:
- Keeping the map set.
- Always knowing where they are on the map.

- Remembering the thinking sequence . .
  Where am I?
  Where do I want to go?
  How do I get there?

- Deciding in which order they want to find the controls (in this score event).

Hold a mass start (everyone starts together) and the children should complete the score event within the time limit. Each child can add up his/her own score. With nearly all the children gaining maximum scores, the competitive element can be played down. Discussion can take place on route choice. Promote an atmosphere of enjoyment in completing the course to the best of your ability (not simply to beat someone else).

Children who ask if they can do more orienteering could be given an information sheet including the name and address of the local club secretary and the dates of the next local events.

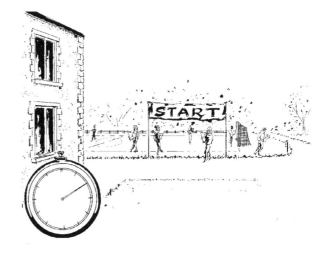

Planning and organisation points

1. Although the mass start and limited time make score events easy to organise and it does not matter if controls are missed, it is more difficult for children to start, easier for them to get lost and more difficult to keep track of them. The choice of area and format and planning of the activity therefore become very important.

Clear instructions must be given on what to do if time has run out and they are lost - collecting features should be indicated (e.g. central forest road) and whistles given out with an emergency procedure. The start/finish should always be on a forest road or path.

2. Score orienteering can test and reinforce every technique, but control points should be carefully chosen to avoid offering 'fine' orienteering beyond the capabilities of the children or risks of approaching hazards like steep crags or deep streams.

Evaluation

Score competitions provide excellent opportunities for post-event discussions and analyses - particularly on order of visiting controls and route choice. Children should be encouraged to discuss their routes between controls and exchange maps. Emphasise -

'Where are you?
Where did you want to go?
How did you get there?

Check that they are now all orientating their map with the compass as a matter of habit and holding the map looking along the direction of travel.

Microcomputing and orienteering

Does your school have a microcomputer? Software exists that may enable you to link what your children have been learning in their orienteering programme to the computer. Take advantage of this opportunity to allow your class to familiarise themselves with the scope of the computer by playing educational games currently available and suitable for primary use.

A software package (OCAD) gives teachers the opportunity to draw their own maps, allowing easy reproduction and updating. If a school cannot afford OCAD the local LEA may be able to help by assisting the production of maps for groups of schools. Professional mappers also offer the facility of putting a school map on disk. Older children can be introduced to the computer mapping process as well as using computers for results and event organisation. For mapping guidance, see Appendix E.

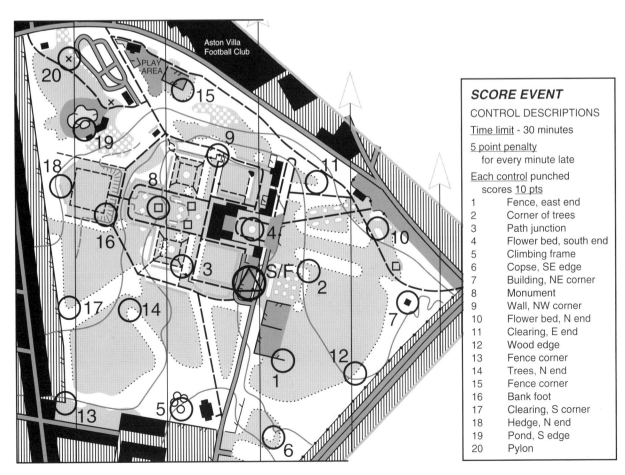

SCORE EVENT

CONTROL DESCRIPTIONS

Time limit - 30 minutes

5 point penalty
  for every minute late

Each control punched
  scores 10 pts

1	Fence, east end
2	Corner of trees
3	Path junction
4	Flower bed, south end
5	Climbing frame
6	Copse, SE edge
7	Building, NE corner
8	Monument
9	Wall, NW corner
10	Flower bed, N end
11	Clearing, E end
12	Wood edge
13	Fence corner
14	Trees, N end
15	Fence corner
16	Bank foot
17	Clearing, S corner
18	Hedge, N end
19	Pond, S edge
20	Pylon

14 LINE ORIENTEERING
IN THE GYMNASIUM/HALL

OBJECTIVES
- *To revise map to ground observation*
- *Running and team activity*
- *To develop understanding of the following terms:*
  LINE ORIENTEERING, MINI MAPS, TEAM

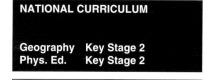

NATIONAL CURRICULUM

Geography	Key Stage 2
Phys. Ed.	Key Stage 2

EQUIPMENT
Gym apparatus
Maps
Pencils or crayons
Mini maps for each team of 3-4

Teacher preparation
Lay out a simple pattern of apparatus. Draw a plan and copy for each pupil, or ask the pupils to draw in the shapes themselves. Mark the north side with a colour.

Practical
Each pupil creates a line which shows an interesting route weaving around (or under or over) the apparatus. Draw the line and follow it round. Hold the map with two hands out in front and let it 'steer' you around. Keep it set all the time. Use the north side of the area to set the map. Swop maps and follow someone else's line.

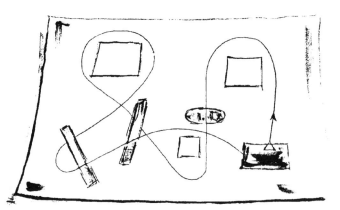

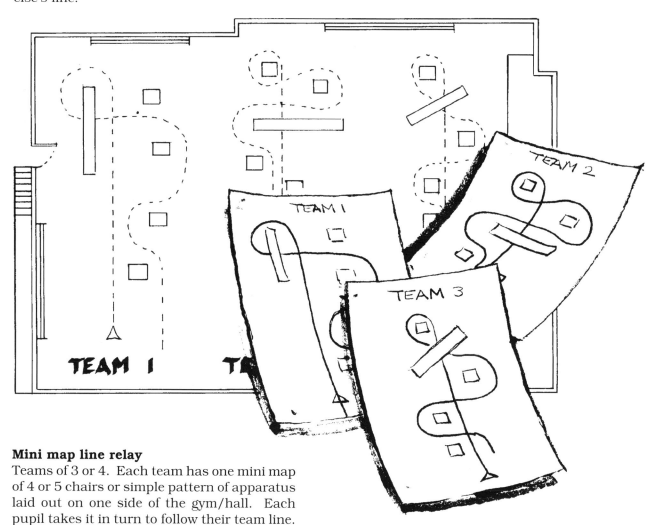

Mini map line relay
Teams of 3 or 4. Each team has one mini map of 4 or 5 chairs or simple pattern of apparatus laid out on one side of the gym/hall. Each pupil takes it in turn to follow their team line. When every team has finished each team moves on to the next position. NB There are *no* winners or losers.

LESSON 15 LINE ORIENTEERING
IN PARK OR WOODLAND

OBJECTIVES
- *To encourage continuous map contact*
- *Thumbing the map*
- *Individual decision making*
- *Sustained running activity*
- *To specify locations and movement from angles on the map and route*
- *To develop understanding of the following terms:*
  THUMBING, CONCENTRATION, MAP CONTACT

NATIONAL CURRICULUM
Geography   Key Stage 2 & 3
Phys. Ed.   Key Stage 2 & 3
Mathematics Key Stage 2 & 3
+ Environmental Education

EQUIPMENT
Pencils (on string)
Maps
Controls

Teacher Preparation

Plan a circular route following line features (mainly paths) with lots of changes of direction. This should be about 800m long, not more, because of the level of concentration required to follow it. Put out 3-6 control markers at distinctive points along the route.

The first control should be near the beginning of the line. Mark up the maps with a red line showing the route the children have to follow. Do not mark the controls on the map. Children find this type of exercise quite hard because they are used to running freely until they see the flag. In this exercise they have to read the map all the time.

Assistant: Puts out controls. Helps children to follow the line.

Lesson

1. Use a short map walk to familiarise the group with the map and surrounding terrain. Revise setting the map. Explain the purpose of the lesson. Each pupil

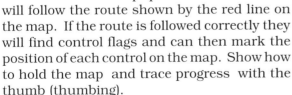

will follow the route shown by the red line on the map. If the route is followed correctly they will find control flags and can then mark the position of each control on the map. Show how to hold the map and trace progress with the thumb (thumbing).

2. Thumb the start and take the whole group along the line to the first control. Mark the position of this control accurately on the maps. Use language associated with angles when appropriate.

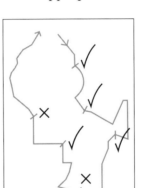

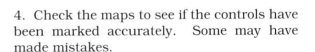

3. Allow the more able to continue on their own to the next control. If they mark that correctly then let them continue round to the finish and wait there. Continue behind with the remainder of the group sending them ahead as they become more competent and their confidence increases.

4. Check the maps to see if the controls have been marked accurately. Some may have made mistakes.

5. Go round the route again with the whole group together. Check that the children are in contact with the map at each control marker. Practise looking at the map as you walk or run along. Thumbing the map helps to do this quickly.

6. Before collecting the markers have a running race round the same route.

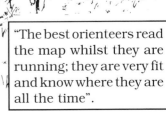

"The best orienteers read the map whilst they are running; they are very fit and know where they are all the time".

Adaptations

1 The course can be made more challenging by varying the route of the line. It can start off very easy following paths and then cut path corners and go past smaller features in the woods or it can wind round obvious contour features like small hills. It can thereby be used to teach the particular skills which are relevant to the children's experience.

2 The positioning of the controls can be adapted to skills levels, e.g. positioning on a straight path or bank. Penalty points can be adapted to millimetres 'out' on the map.

3 In addition to marking the locations of markers on the line, pupils can also write down an appropriate control description.

4 For very young or less able pupils tapes can be put out on more difficult sections of the course, or the whole course can be marked by streamers or continuous string. The children can simply 'punch' at each marker, or draw the position of each marker on their map as they reach it. As well as teaching safe navigation on school sites, String Events on this model are very popular with young children at many BOF events. Variations on the idea are also used to provide orienteering competition experience for children with mental and physical disabilities under the generic title of Trail Orienteering.

By marking a route on paths through benign terrain, the 'string' concept can offer a countryside adventure experience to children of all ages and levels of ability. If more challenge is required the markers can be placed just off the string which can then be used simply as a safety handrail.

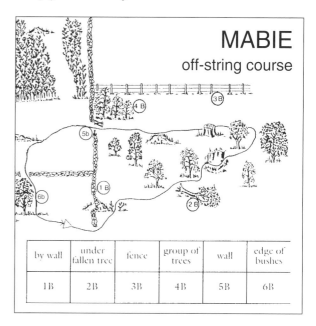

by wall	under fallen tree	fence	group of trees	wall	edge of bushes
1B	2B	3B	4B	5B	6B

5 If the course is short, the pupils can be given a run round a second time to show how fast they could have done it, or a 3 person running relay can use the three loops.

Evaluation

The children can discuss their performance in pairs discussing why controls were missed, why they left the line and whether they could have used any back-up skills like compass and pacing to improve their accuracy.

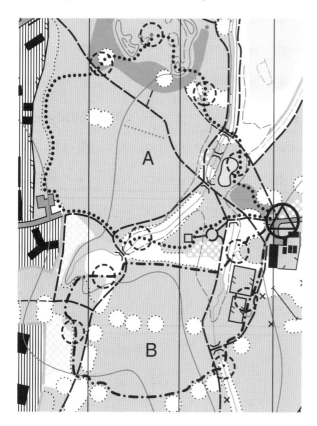

<table>
<tr><td>

LESSON

16

</td><td>

ROUTE CHOICE (+ HANDRAILS, MAP COPYING)
IN PARK OR WOODLAND

OBJECTIVES
- *To emphasise the importance of choosing a route*
- *To show the advantages of using line features as handrails*
- *To understand scale and distance*
- *The use of networks to solve problems*
- *Decision making*
- *Environmental awareness*
- *To develop understanding of the following terms:*
  HANDRAILS, ROUTE CHOICE, LINE FEATURES, SCALE

</td><td>

NATIONAL CURRICULUM
Geography   Key Stage 2 & 3
Phys. Ed.   Key Stage 2 & 3
Mathematics Key Stage 2 & 3
+ Environmental & Social Education

EQUIPMENT
Maps and route choice card game
Control markers and codes
Control cards and punches/crayons
Pens
Safety pins

</td></tr>
</table>

Teacher Preparation

Collect a variety of maps and make up cards with one route choice problem on each card. Cover the cards with transparent film. Each route should include 2-4 different line features linking each pair of controls. Number the cards, and include scale and legend on the back.

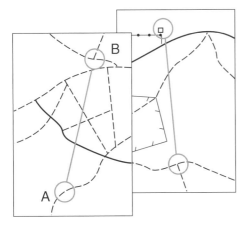

Route choice card game

Select an area where you could set up a star exercise with 2-3 features linking the base to each control. Make three Master Maps showing all controls and the Base/Start. Include a list of control descriptions. Put the start on each map. Controls should be within 250 metres.

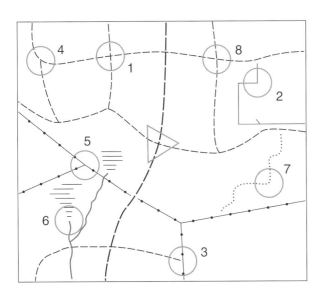

Safety: star exercises take place in a safe contained area with straightforward group management. Ensure the children understand that they must return to base after finding each control.

Assistant: Puts out controls - each having a code letter, and a punch or coloured crayon.

Lesson

1 Use the card game for a school-based lesson to discuss route choice, handrails and scale.

2 In the park or woodland give out control cards. Each pupil pins one to his/her clothing.

3 Explain how the star exercise works. Each participant must return to the start after finding each control. Give each child a number. This is the number of the control that child is to copy and find first. Two or three children at a time copy one control each onto their maps. The teacher checks for accuracy. Each pupil describes the route he/she will take before setting off. A NORTH arrow on the ground will facilitate map setting.

4 As each pupil returns, check the punch mark, then ask the child to copy the next control and its description from the Master Map. Aim for each pupil to visit 3 - 5 controls.

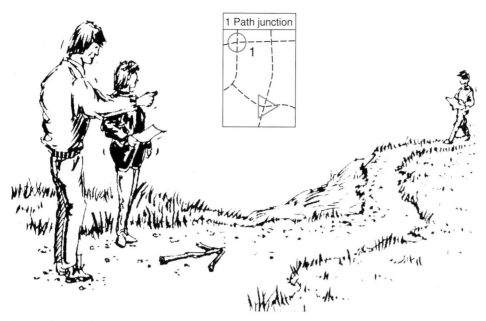

5. At the end have a competition to see who can bring in the controls the fastest: one pair of children per control. They could go out together and return by separate routes. Calculate which was the fastest pair.

Eg. Gary & Angela No 2 250m in 2mins 30secs = 10 minutes per kilometre.

Scale and distance measurement

Use these controls to discuss scale. Measure the distance taken to each control and work out how far it is:

Map 1:5,000: 1millimetre (mm) = 5 metres (m) so distance to Control 1 = 20mm = 100m

Map 1:10,000: 1mm = 10 metres so distance to control 1 = 20mm = 200m

A more advanced Route Choice exercise (Key Stages 2 or 3) on an orienteering map of a local park.

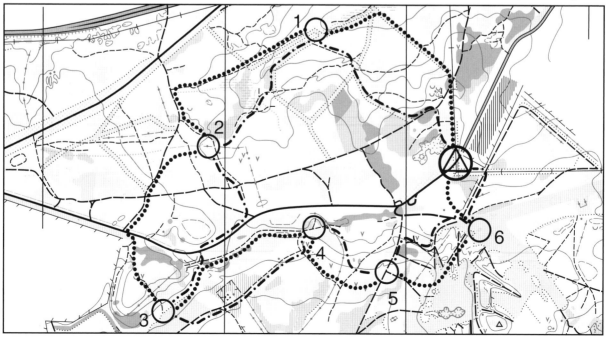

LESSON
17

INTRODUCING THE COMPASS
IN THE CLASSROOM

NATIONAL CURRICULUM
Geography   Key Stage 2 & 3
Phys. Ed.   Key Stage 2
Mathematics Key Stage 2 & 3
+ Environmental & Social Education

OBJECTIVES
* *To introduce the compass as an aid to navigation*
* *To understand and use bearings to define directions*
* *To develop understanding of the following terms:*
  MAP NORTH, MAGNETIC NORTH, COMPASS NORTH, PARALLEL

EQUIPMENT
Examples of a map guide compass, a
protractor compass and a thumb compass
Set of compasses (one for each pupil)
Direction cards

Teacher preparation
Display the four types of compass (see next page) and a large labelled diagram.

Make up a set of cards with the eight cardinal directions marked.

 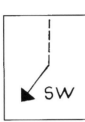 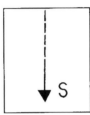

Direction cards

Lesson

1 Show the four types of compass to the class and explain the principles upon which the magnetic compass works, including some of its history, development and applications

2 Distribute a set of compasses. Examine the compasses and discuss the parts.

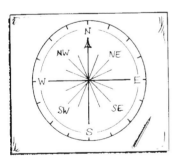

3 The pupils draw a compass and label it.

4 Design and draw a compass rose showing the eight cardinal points.

5 Use the compass to find Magnetic North in the room, then determine each of the other cardinal points. Include language associated with angles.

6 Each child draws a plan of his/her desk and uses the compass to mark North-South lines on the plan. Draw several parallel lines indicating map north.

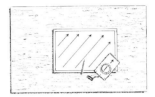

7. Allow further opportunities for establishing the cardinal directions within the classroom.

8. Move to a hall or larger area and use the set of direction cards. Ensure each child has a card. Indicate which side of the area is North. The children run round swopping cards at frequent intervals, when the whistle goes each pupil runs to the corner or side indicated on the card. Show them how to set the card to North to find the correct direction.

Orienteering compasses

The compass is a direction finding instrument invaluable as an aid to precise navigation. Correct use will allow the orienteer to keep the map orientated in order to select routes and follow them faster while maintaining contact with the map. Maps used for orienteering have only magnetic North lines. This enables the compass to be used easily for map orientation.

Orienteers use four different types of compass:

MAP GUIDE COMPASS

This is designed and recommended to help the beginner to concentrate on looking at and thumbing the map, once it is orientated.

SILVA TYPE 7DNS 'DIRECT' COMPASS

This is a much simplified version of the standard protractor compass, designed especially for children as a result of the Liverpool University Research Project into Children's Navigational Skills. It allows map orientation, direction checking and rough bearings to cut corners or aim off. It is ideal for beginners because the magnetic needle can be seen clearly within the housing and north on the compass dial is highlighted in red. When the red north-pointing magnetic needle matches the red N on the dial, all cardinal points and bearings can be read easily. Just remember, **RED to RED** for orientation. More sophisticated protractor compasses are available, but the 'Direct' compass allows basic skills to be learnt more easily.

PROTRACTOR COMPASS

The protractor compass, like the 'Direct' compass can be used to take bearings as well as set the map. It requires careful teaching and considerable practice to use this compass accurately. Bearings are included as part of lesson 9.

THUMB COMPASS

This is good for older beginners but can be an encumbrance for children; their small hands are needed primarily to hold the map. The single unit (map and compass) helps to focus attention on the map.

It is important that whichever compass is chosen it is used in the correct way and that all the children in a class are taught with the same type of compass.

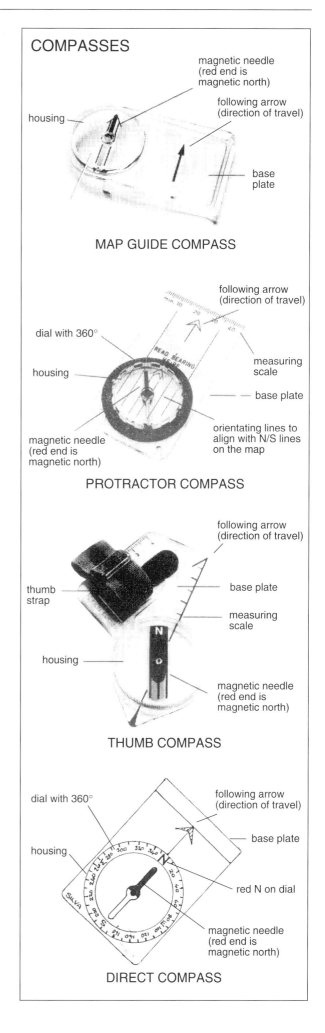

COMPASSES

MAP GUIDE COMPASS

PROTRACTOR COMPASS

THUMB COMPASS

DIRECT COMPASS

<table>
<tr><td>

LESSON

18°

</td><td>

SETTING THE MAP USING A COMPASS
IN SCHOOL GROUNDS OR PARKLAND

</td><td>

NATIONAL CURRICULUM
Geography   Key Stage 2 & 3
Phys. Ed.   Key Stage 2 & 3
Mathematics Key Stage 2 & 3
+ Environmental Education

</td></tr>
</table>

OBJECTIVES
- *To establish that map north and magnetic (compass) north must always match on an orientated map*
- *To practise orienteering using a map and compass*
- *To develop understanding of the following terms:*
  COMPASS, MAP NORTH, MAGNETIC NORTH, COMPASS NORTH

EQUIPMENT
Compasses
Maps
Control cards and pins
Control markers, codes, punches/crayons

Teacher preparation

In a familiar area, prepare a mini-course star exercise with several controls which can be linked from different directions. Make a master map with all the controls on. Mark the pupils' maps with the start and two controls for the group practice.
Assistant: Puts out controls, helps at Start.

Lesson

1 Pin on the control cards then hand out the maps and compasses. If using the map guide compass, show how to clip it to the side of the map.
        Go through the teaching stages given on the next page, then show the group how to set the map with the compass.

2 With the whole group together, visit the two controls on the maps using the compass to set the map at each control. Return to the start.

3 Explain the star exercise. The pupils line up and are given two or three new controls to visit. Mark different mini courses on each pupil's map. Check that the map is set before the child sets off. Assistance is essential with a group of eight or more.

4 Use the last 15 minutes to bring in the control markers.

5 Pupils work out how far they have been during the lesson, eg. 2.5 km in 50 minutes.

Follow up

A variety of compass exercises in the school grounds.

49

Teaching stages

1 Establish NORTH. The magnetic needle always points North-South. Wherever you face, however you twist or turn, the compass needle always points to north.

2 Fold the map square and small enough to 'thumb' your location. Hold the map so that you are looking straight along the route you want to take.

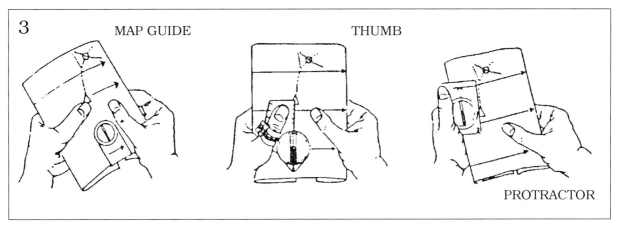

3a MAPGUIDE. Hold the map steady using two hands to 'steer'.

3b THUMB. Place your thumb and the corner of the leading edge at your location. Use the other hand to help hold the map steady at first.

3c PROTRACTOR. Place the edge of the compass alongside the route you want to take. Use two hands to hold the map steady at first.

4 Turn yourself with map and compass fixed in front of you until the magnetic needle lies parallel to North-South lines on the map. Needle North = Map North.

5 You are now facing along the direction line you want to take. Take the spare hand away from the map: off you go! The protractor compass can be held in the opposite hand to the map if preferred.

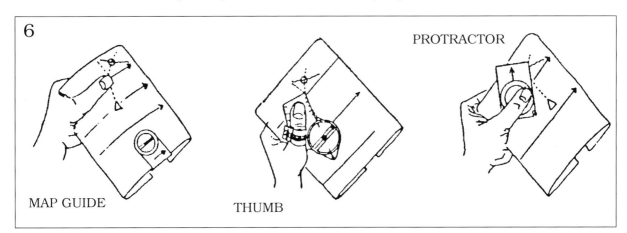

6 Continue to read the map with your thumb. When the path changes direction - move your thumb - turn the map to look straight along the line you want to take - check that the Needle North points to Map North. Check that the map is set all the time and keep it in front of your body.

Points to watch
- Always keep map and compass horizontal to allow the needle to swing freely.
- Hold map and compass about waist level and keep them working together.
- Lots of practice with accurate feedback is essential for understanding.

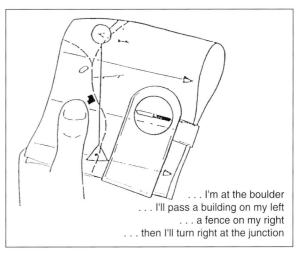

. . . I'm at the boulder
. . . I'll pass a building on my left
. . . a fence on my right
. . . then I'll turn right at the junction

LESSON 19 NAVIGATING BY CONTOURS
IN AN AREA WITH GOOD CONTOUR DETAIL

NATIONAL CURRICULUM
Geography   Key Stage 2 & 3
Phys. Ed.   Key Stage 2 & 3
Mathematics Key Stage 2 & 3
+ Environmental Education

OBJECTIVES
* *To introduce contours as an additional aid to good navigation*
* *To interpret relief*
* *Two dimensional representation of three dimensional objects*
* *To develop understanding of the following terms:*
  CONTOUR LINES, STEEPNESS, SHAPE, UPHILL, DOWNHILL

EQUIPMENT
Maps
Control markers

Teacher Preparation

Give a short introduction to contours in the classroom. Follow with a visit to an area with distinctive contour features. Plan a map walk and a short course (0.5-1km) with control points on contour features. Make up control description lists using contour terms, eg. hill top, foot of steep slope, re-entrant, spur. Pupils will only be able to complete a course on their own if they have already developed confidence in map reading.

Assistant: Patrols the course area and assists with map walk.

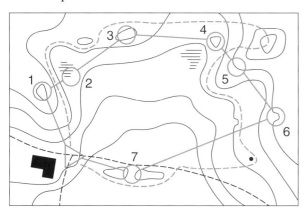

Lesson

1 Map walk: lead the group showing examples of shape and slope.

2 Demonstrate and practice how to set the map by looking at the shape of ground. Navigate to features by using the contours.

3 Go to the start of the course. Set pupils off at intervals. The controls should be quite close together so that the contour feature is distinctive and simple,

e.g. 1-2: Down the hill to the bottom.
      2-3: The second hilltop along.
      3-4: A hill on its own in a flat area.

Have a safety direction and an assistant patrolling the area or helping at the control sites.

4 The children mark up their routes and describe the contour features they used to reach the controls.

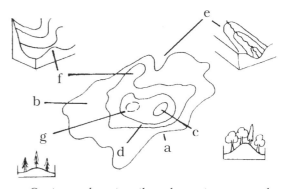

a: Contours close together show steep ground
b: Contours spaced apart show a gradual slope or flatter ground
c: A ring contour shows a hill top
d: The more contours there are, the higher the hill
e: A valley or re-entrant is shown by a bend in a contour pointing to the uphill side. It may or may not have a stream in it
f: A spur or ridge is shown with a nose-shaped contour line
g: A form line (intermediate contour) helps to improve the picture the map gives to the orienteer

Follow up

Make contour models at school.

Use a contour card game . . . .

| LESSON 20 | **PREPARATION FOR FINAL COMPETITION** IN THE CLASSROOM | **NATIONAL CURRICULUM** |

NATIONAL CURRICULUM

| Geography | Key Stage 2 & 3 |
| Phys. Ed. | Key Stage 2 & 3 |

OBJECTIVES
- *To familiarise everyone with the park/woodland map to be used in lesson 20*
- *To give information on local events and the local orienteering club*
- *To provide an opportunity for social education, fair competition, environmental awareness*
- *To develop understanding of the following terms:*
  CONTOURS, ORIENTEERING CLUB, BADGES

EQUIPMENT
Park/woodland maps covered with
   adhesive film
Photocopies of the same map
Local club handout and fixture list
Spirit-based red pens (fine tip)

Preparation

Cover coloured maps with adhesive film. Plan 1 or 2 courses for lesson 20; one can be slightly longer but both must be really easy because of the unfamiliar terrain, eg. 1.0-1.5km with 8 to 12 controls. All controls should be linked by only one line feature on each leg. In open parkland each control should be visible from the previous one.

Permanent courses: if a permanent course is to be used, prepare the maps in the same way. The pupils can then link the controls to be visited with a red line.

Assistance: arrange for parents or other adults to assist (do not presume that they can read a map). Attendance at this preparation lesson would be useful.

Lesson

• Give a copy of the coloured map to each pupil, plus a photocopy. The coloured maps can be used many times if they are covered with clear adhesive film and a permanent felt tip used to draw in circles and routes. Methylated spirit will remove felt tip marks easily.

• Practise copying the course from a master map on to the coloured map unless it is already pre-marked.

• Route description exercises - verbal or written

• CONTOURS - if there are any on the map, discuss their purpose. They won't be seen on the ground! so they can't be followed like a track!

• Key - look for examples of the different symbols with an emphasis on line features and colours. Play a game or organise a quiz to improve familiarity with the key.

Discuss

The plan for next lesson:
Outing to the park/woodland.
Equipment and clothing. Food?
Criteria for the starting order.

Rules and safety:
Use of whistle only in emergency.
Everyone MUST REPORT TO THE FINISH.
No shouting or calling.
No litter.
Controls must be found in the right order.

How to carry on orienteering - local club.
Events always open to beginners (handout).

Fixtures
Colour-coded courses are most common. Progress through the colours, which increase in difficulty - White - Yellow - Orange - Red - Green - Blue - Brown. The course for lesson 21 will be of white or yellow standard. Some events you enter according to your age and sex, eg M10 or W10 for boys and girls aged 10 years or under.

Fixture lists can be obtained from your local club or regional fixtures secretary through the British Orienteering Federation. In addition there are many schools associations which arrange their own fixtures, often on a team basis, eg the London and Liverpool Panathlons, or through membership of the British Schools Orienteering Association which publishes a termly magazine, Search, with a full schools fixture list, news and information on orienteering resources. As well as regional and local schools leagues and competitions there are two national team and individual schools championships each autumn. The BSOA event is on the score principle while the BOF British Schools Championship is the more conventional point to point event. Both events attract four figure entries. Further details from BOF or BSOA.

Badge schemes
Some regions have their own badge schemes to encourage participation, eg Scotland - a badge when 5, 10 and 20 events have been completed. The colour-coded badge scheme is administered by local clubs. To gain a colour badge you must finish 3 courses of the same colour in the top half of those who started or within one and a half times the winner's time. Pairs can also qualify for colour awards.

Keep the coloured maps but let the children take the photocopy home to look at.

<table>
<tr><td>LESSON
21</td><td>**FINAL COMPETITION**
IN LOCAL PARK OR WOODLAND</td></tr>
</table>

NATIONAL CURRICULUM
Geography   Key Stage 2 & 3
Phys. Ed.   Key Stage 2 & 3
Mathematics Key Stage 2 & 3
Cross curricular

OBJECTIVES
• *To give a taste of real orienteering*
• *To complete the series of lessons*
• *To provide opportunities for cross curricular work - environmental education,*
   social education, design technology, language
• *To develop understanding of the following terms:*
   LINE FEATURE, ROUTE CHOICE, MAP COLOURS, POINT TO POINT EVENT

EQUIPMENT
Premarked maps, description and code lists
Control cards, safety pins, pencils
Full size control markers + punches/crayons
Tapes for marking walk, clock, compasses
Compasses, whistles, waterproofs

1 MAP WALK. This is essential before starting the competition. Take the group for a map walk following a pre-marked route. Point out features and revise map setting. Look at contours if they are on the map. Indicate changes of vegetation (colour). Highlight the line features they will have to follow on the course. Use the sun in the south to set the map. The map walk should finish at the START area for the competition.

2 Give a start order and times. Encourage individual participation and a positive attitude. Emphasise that they should do their best to find all the controls.

3 Before starting, pin control card and descriptions to clothing. Start time to be written on the card.

4 Using a one-minute start interval set them off. If there are two courses, two can start at once. POINT TO POINT COURSE 1.0km - 1.5km, estimated time will be 12 - 30 minutes.

5 FINISH. Set up a timing system at the same time as the start. Put any spare staff or parents out at one or two controls, suggest that they only offer advice if asked for or if the pupil is obviously going the wrong way.

6 RESULTS. Calculate results and display. Praise all those who found all the controls. Add time on for each control missed rather than disqualify. Early finishers can help with the results. A plan should be made beforehand to cope with the possibility of someone getting lost. They should be told to stay on a track or path somewhere in the area.

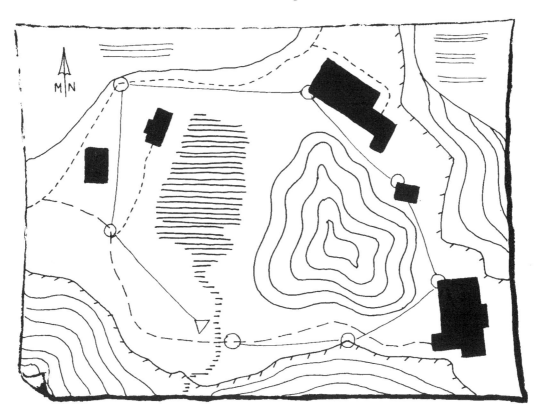

Safety
Consideration of the area and the amount of help available will influence how independent the pupils can be. Make sure everyone knows where the base is (eg car park) and that they should return there when they finish.

Getting lost - emergency signal. In outdoor adventurous activities the emergency signal for someone completely lost or injured and requiring help is 6 long blasts on the whistle repeated at one minute intervals. The response by the searcher is 3 short blasts.

ALTERNATIVE

Introduction
Another version of a final competition to discourage 'following' is to plan a series of loop courses on a school or park map as shown below. Permutating a scatter of controls into simple courses in this way is not as difficult as it sounds.

Teacher preparation
Plan 4 point to point courses with 5 controls each. Make 2 master maps of each course, label them A, B, C, and D - colour code them, eg A red, B blue, C green, D brown.

Make up one map with all the controls on and use to put out controls and punches/crayons. If pupils are to put controls out photocopy this map x 20 and highlight one control site on each map (no codes or descriptions will encourage accuracy of copying and finding correct controls).

Make a master control card for each course.

Lesson/Practical Exercises
Organise the pupils to put out controls if using a familiar area. Emphasise accuracy and show how to tie them securely. Canes may need to be used. Pupils return to base. The teacher checks as many controls as possible whilst they are being hung.

Give out maps and compasses and control cards (pin to waist or arm).

8 pupils start together - 2 on A, 2 on B, etc. They copy the course onto their map using coloured pens.

Start the next 8 after 2 minutes or as soon as a master map is clear. Controls must be found in the correct order 1 - 5.

Once completed, each pupil checks the punch patterns with the master card then copies the next course using a different coloured pen.

The competition can be to see who can find the most controls and punch or mark the control card accurately, i.e. 20 = maximum correct controls. If time is limited, compete over only 2 or 3 courses.

Leave time to discuss routes and skills learnt.

Teaching points
Check accuracy of copying controls.

Orientate map and select route at each control.

Know what feature you are looking for. The fit map readers will make the best orienteers.

Further work
One or two point to point courses in a local park will be challenging at this stage and more appropriate at key stage 4. Pre-marked maps will save time and ease lesson organisation especially if it is wet.

Plan courses at yellow standard emphasising following line features to find controls but introducing a variety of 'handrails' if possible (e.g. field edges, streams or earth banks as well as paths).

Give out the maps and get the pupils to decide which handrails they will use. Then send them round the course to follow the routes they have chosen.

Evaluation
If the pupils have set out control markers in pairs they will have been evaluating their own map reading accuracy.

In any case, do not presume that the whole group will have taken in everything first time. Use opportunities afterwards for discussion and feedback. Encourage children to discuss their courses and routes.

If other maps with courses are available to pass round and discuss routes, so much the better. Suitable questions might be - "Which way did you choose between 1 and 2? - Did you cut any corners? - Did you use yor compass?" The greater their familiarity with maps, the faster will their mapreading progress.

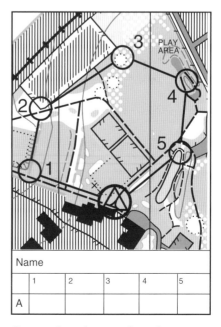

Course A with control card

COURSE PLANNING GUIDELINES

1 The start should be on a distinctive line feature on map and ground e.g. track junction. The start order can be 'drawn out of a hat' to give a bit of fun. Control cards and descriptions can be pinned to clothing before the start and the start time written on control card.

2 All control points must be on precise map and ground features.

3 The controls must correspond with the centre of a red circle about 5mm in diameter. Always draw with a circle template.

4 Beginners like plenty of controls linked by distinctive line features (e.g. 10-12 on a 3 km course).

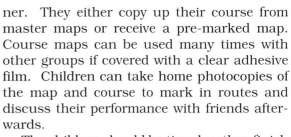

5 Controls should be seen if approached from any direction and never hidden in depressions, bushes or behind a tree. 'Above ground' features make the best sites for beginners.

6 Avoid 'dog-legs' which involve going in and coming out of a control the same way. This encourages 'following' and gives controls away.

Avoid dog legs

7 Don't use impossible or dangerous legs which involve thick undergrowth on a direct route or going near dangerous roads, walls, cliffs, etc.

8 Select a size of marker to suit the terrain - 10cm square for school grounds. 30cm square in woodland. Hang punches or pencils on a separate cane to avoid damage to the marker.

9 Vary the length of legs and control features in point to point orienteering.

10 In a score orienteering event (which is a good model for covering a wide range of abilities), controls should be evenly distributed and easy to find. Number controls so as to discourage visiting them in the order 1 - 20, and if points values are allocated accordingly to difficulty, do not group high scoring controls together.

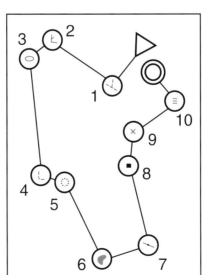

Vary the length and direction of legs and the control features

Practical exercise
The children compete individually at 1 minute intervals, the fastest back being the win-

ner. They either copy up their course from master maps or receive a pre-marked map. Course maps can be used many times with other groups if covered with a clear adhesive film. Children can take home photocopies of the map and course to mark in routes and discuss their performance with friends afterwards.

The children should be timed as they finish and their results made available as soon as possible. Parents are sometimes useful in helping at start and finish and patrolling the course to give help if required.

Organisation points
1 Prepare the children thoroughly beforehand explaining the system and pointing out parts of the course where special care is needed - e.g. new paths or vague areas on map or ground. Encourage a positive attitude.

2 Go through the control descriptions to ensure that the children know what they are looking for.

3 Pin control card and descriptions to clothing (waist level) to allow easy attention to the map.

4 Make sure that clothing/footwear are adequate for the terrain.

5 Explain safety procedures e.g. use whistle only in emergency (6 blasts). Everyone must report to the finish and be quite clear where it is. No shouting or calling. Safety bearing if appropriate, etc.

6 On point to point courses, stress that controls must be visited in the right order.

7 Emphasise respect for the countryside e.g. no litter, gates to be closed etc.

8 Give out information on local fixture lists and incentive schemes. If an orienteer from the local club can be present so much the better.

9 Try not to disqualify anyone. Praise all those who found all the controls without too much trouble and add time for each control missed. A short presentation to the winners can be fun too.

5 Assessing Orienteering Activities within the National Curriculum

The teaching and learning of orienteering cannot be separated from assessment. It is an important and inter-related part of the process and should not be regarded as an 'add-on' activity. Assessment has two essential purposes. First, it should tell us about individual progress, i.e. what a particular child has learned and achieved. Second, it should assist the teacher in evaluating the teaching methods, content and organisation, and provide a basis for forward planning.

There is also a third element. Assessment is diminished if the results are not communicated. Knowing how the young orienteer has performed not only allows accurate feedback and positive reinforcement to be given but also puts the teacher in a position to inform other interested parties. We all need to know how we are doing and how improvements can be made. Assessment aids this process.

Assessment should be continuous and conducted during the teaching activities. It should be concerned with what a child knows and can do, seen against a Statement of Attainment (SoA) reflected in End of Key Stage or Level Descriptions

THE INFORM PROCESS

The Schools Examination and Assessment Council (SEAC) have produced a six step process of teacher assessment called INFORM. Though printed below as a list the process should be seen in the round. There is no first or last step.

Identify Statements of Attainment your lesson plans will promote

Note carefully opportunities for the child to demonstrate attainment

Focus on the performance, looking for evidence of attainment

Offer the child the chance to discuss what has been achieved

Record what you have identified as noteworthy

Modify future lesson plans for the child accordingly

Dearing made assessment much less prescriptive and time consuming. Record keeping is now a professional matter for school and teacher which is seen as a means to an end and therefore should keep paper and time to a minimum. It should not interfere with the process of teaching.

Essentially these statements say simply that assessment should be continuous and conducted during teaching activities; that end of Key Stage descriptions should be used as reference points; and that teacher and pupils should be working together in evaluating achievement and making judgements on how to improve skills and performance.

In orienteering terms competitive results can, of course, define the success or otherwise of teaching and learning but it is important too to assess which skills have been learnt and performed correctly and which not (eg use of compass). Because much of orienteering activity takes place out of sight of the teacher it is important that pupils themselves assess their own performance and discuss with friends and teacher their successes and mistakes as well as personal programmes for improvement. Let us now look at some examples of assessment in an orienteering context.

EXAMPLE 1
Geographical Skills Programme of Study 'Use maps and plans at a variety of scales to follow routes'.

Content: The content relates to many of the progressive activities set out in the lessons in Chapter 4, and in particular to numbers 2, 3, 4, 5, 6, 7, 9, 10, 11, 12, 14, 15, 16 and 19.

Context: The teaching has been arranged to equip the young orienteer to follow a route or a trail around the school playground or site using a map which might have been produced by the teacher, another adult or a child. The children are now ready to be tested.

The assessment task raises three questions for the teacher:

Q1 Is the task relevant to a particular SoA?

Q2 Is the response of the child appropriate to the SoA?

Q3 How many times should the child demonstrate the attainment of this kind of activity?

It is clear that the answer to question one is Yes. But how do we judge a child's response? The key is to make systematic observations of an individual. It may mean that on this occasion other children are not monitored. Equally, the children could be assessed in turn.

There is also a need to be clear about the evidence to be gathered. What constitutes a successful response? The criteria need to be agreed beforehand. For example, is it acceptable for the child to complete the task if he took one wrong turn at a junction but then corrected himself? Is it acceptable if the child completed the route but did not maintain contact with the map by using a thumbing technique?

The incident of the wrong turn, though corrected, might mean that you require the child to demonstrate competence in a new situation. With regard to not keeping map contact, though we as orienteers know this is a desirable technique, it is not necessary for the SoA. The evidence is that the child followed the correct path thus achieving the objective. Both situations raise the question as to how much evidence should be gathered and whether this should be in more than one situation.

Regardless of the outcome it is important to record how the child performed and use the information as a reference point for future tests. The careful observation of how the child carried out the task, i.e. not keeping map contact, can also be used to decided when this technique should be introduced.

In order to interpret the evidence correctly it is helpful to give the child the chance to discuss what happened. You can put questions such as "I saw you make a mistake at the path junction but you corrected yourself. How did you do that?" or "I see you completed the route successfully but you hardly seemed to keep track of where you where. How did you do it so well?" The teacher helps the child by describing what he did and can confirm the progress made or explain how help can be given.

In this example the evidence was gained by systematic observation of one pupil at a time against an agreed criteria. The progress of the child can be recorded and if repeated in novel situations, can be seen to match the Statement of Attainment.

Now let us consider an alternative example. In this situation the teacher has conducted an activity and dwells on the children's response. The activity is cross curricular and more demanding than example one.

EXAMPLE 2

This exercise relates to lessons 5, 10 and 16 and draws on the children's experiences as they undertake the activities and the ensuing discussion.

Let us imagine that the children in the class have experience of cross country type events in the school grounds. The teacher now sets them a task to be conducted in pairs. The children, A and B, individually plan a 4 control cross country event with an agreed start and finish point. They write control descriptions for each other. The control sites and descriptions are checked by the teacher and the controls are set out.

A now tackles B's course and vice versa. Afterwards they discuss the courses they set, the problems involved and the accuracy of the control sites. Time was not taken in this instance. The emphasis was on course setting, the location of the controls, accurate descriptions and finding the controls. The compass was used throughout to maintain orientation.

Let us apply the INFORM framework again. The first act is to identify the SoA. This time there are several, spanning across four subject areas.

Geography	Use a large-scale map to locate their own position and features outside the classroom
Maths	Use the 8 points of the compass to show direction
Maths	Specify location
Maths	Identify and obtain information necessary to solve problems

Statements of Attainment related to a point to point orienteering exercise

Key Stage 2 PE (general)	Respond safely, alone (and with others) to challenging tasks.
	Evaluate how well they and others perform and behave against criteria suggested by the teacher and suggest ways of improving performance
Key Stage 2 PE (specific)	Experience competitions, inclu- luding those they make up them- selves
	Experience outdoor and adven- turous activities that involve nav- igation
	Be taught the skills necessary for the activity undertaken
English	Relate a real event in a connected narrative which conveys mean- ing to a group of pupils
English	Give a detailed oral account of an event - explain with reasons why a particular course of action was taken.

There are multiple SoA in four curricular areas to attend to here. The SoA do serve as meas- ures against which learning can be judged and they do indicate what evidence to look for to see if achievement matches the target. However, the problem is where to focus. The tasks are conducted in a sequence and in theory it should be possible, but the reality may be problematic. The advantage is that several attainment targets are being addressed within a meaningful context.

A variety of different forms of evidence is being generated.

- *symbolic* ... control sites, start and finish

- *written/symbolic* ... control description sheet

- *practical* ... correct location of controls

- *practical* ... completion of course

- *oral* ... discussion of results

- *oral* ... comparison of performance

Overload can be the problem but the key to assessment is the clear understanding which the teacher will have of the structure of the SoAs underlying the individual children's re- sponse to the task.

Recording can then be made against the individual's name in each of the subject areas. The advantage is that multiple targets have been assessed in one task. The disadvan-

tage is that considerable recording is neces- sary.

The assessment described above is formative (ongoing) and serves diagnostic, evaluative and information purposes. Eventu- ally we reach the point when the overall achieve- ment of the child has to be assessed. This can take place at the end of a Key Stage.

Finally, what problems might you encoun- ter in assessment?

First let us be aware that children's perform- ance does differ from day to day so we must be careful to interpret the evidence. If the topic, skill, or activity does not show confident at- tainment then a repeated assessment may be necessary.

Second, as assessors we need to be clear about what is being assessed and what constitutes the necessary evidence to state that an SoA has been achieved. It is important to discuss this with colleagues and reach agreement as to what constitutes success.

As the young orienteers become more confident the nature of the tasks they tackle grows in complexity and may require them to work collaboratively, eg completing a team score event, or planning an activity for others.

Assessing collaborative effort is diffi- cult. An overview can be taken but individual efforts within the activity will need to be noted. We should ask ourselves "What are the posi- tive contributions of this child at this mo- ment?" and "How are they perceived by the group?"

Records need to be kept but equally, balances have to be struck regarding the amount of detail and frequency of the assess- ment and the evidence to be gathered to allow a summative (end stage) assessment to be made.

Assessment seen in these terms is com- plex. Since orienteering is not a subject within the National Curriculum but a potential vehi- cle for cross curricular activity, the assess- ment, and subsequent recording and report- ing, could be daunting, but it needn't be.

Many of the activities will be practical skills, observable and open to discussion. As such they can be assessed. The teacher who understands the inter-relatedness of the ap- propriate SoAs will possess a clarity which will enable judgements to be made even if the final assessment gives an overview rather than detail on each skill or performance area. If the discussion of the activities is shared with the participants and other teachers then reliable and valid judgements can be made which will benefit the teaching and further progress of the children.

A simple assessment sheet for an orienteering exercise could look like that below:

ORIENTEERING ASSESSMENT: Key Stage 2

- devise and adapt strategies and tactics
- adapt and refine existing skills
- appreciate personal strengths and weaknesses and ways of improving

Pupil Name	Map Orientation	Thumbing	Use of Handrails	Confident Use of Map and Compass to Complete Course
John Adams	√	x	√	?
Nat Barton	√	√	√	√
Jane Cross	√	√	x	x
James Dean	x	x	√	√
Lisa Ferry	√	√	√	√
Graham Green	√	?	√	√

6 A Community Project

Let us now assume that the pupils are confident in the basic skills and knowledgeable and experienced in a particular location, say the school grounds. How can this work be extended and present benefits for others? Is it possible to generate a project which allows the benefits of orienteering to be given to the local community while presenting children at Key Stages 2 and 3 with a real challenge which would embrace other curricular areas?

SETTING UP AN ORIENTEERING COURSE IN A LOCAL PARK

Taking part in an orienteering event requires one level of skill, but making maps, setting problems for others, and monitoring and evaluating the activity raises the level of skill to a much higher standard.

There are many things that pupils could do. They could set line, point to point or score events for other pupils within their own class or within the school. If that was successful, they could put on a small scale event for another school in the locality. However, the scheme we now consider takes orienteering into the community. It is ambitious but not beyond the scope of primary children. It involves the setting up of a number of controls - say 20 to 30 - in a local area, and the production of a map which will be made available to the public. The aim would be to explore the area, locate the controls and receive feedback and reward for the completion of the activity, the whole being organised and/or administered by the school.

The controls could form either a cross-country course or score course, as described earlier. However, we can suggest a further variation - a TRIM event. This event originated in Sweden. The TRIM event challenges individuals, groups and families to use the map to find all the controls marked on it. There is no time limit. It could be completed in a day or over a number of visits to the area.

On completion of the course the control card, which was obtained with the map from the school, is returned and checked. Certificates can be awarded according to success.

The actual control sites could be signs or even nesting boxes high on trees but visible from pathways. Code letters and numbers could be painted on the sides. If markers were used, these could be relocated after a period of time to present new challenges.

The figure opposite shows how the core and foundation subjects are linked by the cross-curricular skills, themes and dimensions to present an integrated topic web. Each aspect of the web is shown in the chart on page 62 in greater detail.

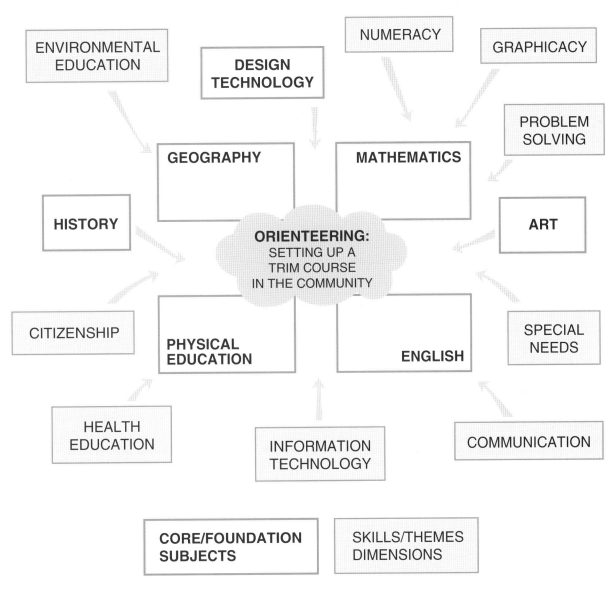

ENVIRONMENTAL EDUCATION

NUMERACY

GRAPHICACY

DESIGN TECHNOLOGY

GEOGRAPHY

MATHEMATICS

PROBLEM SOLVING

HISTORY

ORIENTEERING: SETTING UP A TRIM COURSE IN THE COMMUNITY

ART

CITIZENSHIP

PHYSICAL EDUCATION

ENGLISH

SPECIAL NEEDS

HEALTH EDUCATION

INFORMATION TECHNOLOGY

COMMUNICATION

CORE/FOUNDATION SUBJECTS

SKILLS/THEMES DIMENSIONS

Cross curricular links in an orienteering project

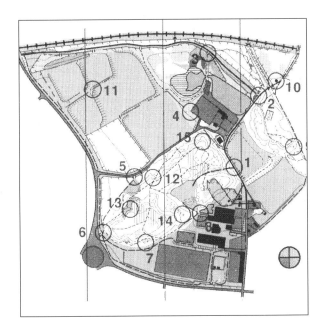

SUMMARY

This topic is challenging but realistic. You may be able to adapt the idea for your own school grounds. Orienteering equips you with skills to tackle problems and challenges within unknown terrain. The community project would present opportunities and difficulties to be solved, but if accomplished would provide considerable benefit to local people and great satisfaction to the instigators. It would be a big step, but you are not alone, for you now have a map (of the curriculum) to guide you.

Some of the contributions of orienteering to aspects of learning and cross curricular competencies are shown overleaf.

Left: Madeley Court Community School Permanent orienteering course

GEOGRAPHY
- Survey the area, check features on the ground
- Extract information from existing maps
- Draw maps
- Decide location of controls

MATHEMATICS
- Use compass and scale to check the position of features
- Consider scale for the maps, having concern for users
- Collect, interpret and present data on use of the course over a trial period

COMMUNICATION
- Develop the basic idea through discussion
- Persuade and negotiate for permission
- Write instructions for the event
- Produce press handout, publicity material
- Report the progress of the venture
- Role play to explore how people will react
- Interview participants who test the event
- Produce questionnaire on reaction to the event
- Tape-record immediate reaction
- Word process the report

HISTORY
- Explore existing maps
- Discuss what changes have taken place
- Was it always like this?
- What detail from conventional maps should be excluded ?

DESIGN TECHNOLOGY/EXPRESSIVE AND AESTHETIC CONSIDERATIONS
- Design/produce a map using up to 5 cols.
- Consider siting of title, key, control card, scale and information
- Design and produce control markers
- Design and produce instruction sheet
- Set up a system for the distribution and collection of control cards and instructions
- Agree roles within the organisation
- Produce publicity material, signs, posters and displays advertising the activity
- Design and produce certificates of completion

PROBLEM SOLVING
- Identify potential problems related to people using the facility
- Identify any potential environmental problems

SPECIAL EDUCATIONAL NEEDS
- Consider the problems faced by people with special needs
- Can the map be used by people who have to walk with aids, the wheelchair bound, the young or the elderly?

INFORMATION TECHNOLOGY
- Set up a database of users

CITIZENSHIP
- Encourage a sense of fair play, a sense of responsibility to others for the management of the event and participation within it

ENVIRONMENTAL
- Discuss the need for maintenance of the course and equipment
- Encourage adherence to the Country Code and good behaviour in the countryside

HEALTH AND FITNESS
- Consider the safety implications of the activity for different abilities and age ranges
- Consider the health and fitness benefits from regular exercise

7 Games

Introduction

The new edition of 'Teaching Orienteering' provides a variety of games, exercises and work programmes which cover the improvement of basic orienteering skills. These include the complete spectrum of the National Curriculum and elements from selected outdoor exercises cab be combined with indoor activities to form classroom projects and modular courses at Key Stages 1, 2 and 3. These could include course planning, mapping and the organisation of orienteering events as well as personal performance. Here we outline three popular indoor games.

1 MATCHING PAIRS

> EQUIPMENT
> Two sheets of different coloured card
> Black, orange, blue, green crayons or felt pens
> Scissors

- Measure out 10 boxes on each sheet of card, each one about 6cm x 8cm.
- Draw in neatly 10 symbols and 10 written descriptions.
- Cut out.

This game can be used by individuals or pairs sitting down and matching the symbols cards with the description cards or as a running game with the cards at different ends of a hall or playground, starting from the middle of the hall.

2 CONTROL FEATURE IDENTIFICATION

> EQUIPMENT
> A variety of orienteering maps
> Circle template, red pen, paper

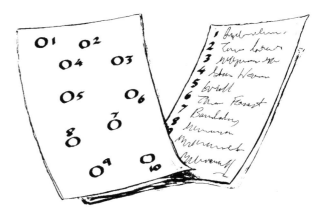

- Select 10 different features - line features plus buildings and colours.
- Draw control circles round each feature.
- Number 1-10 on a piece of paper

The children have to write the correct feature in each circle. This can be done sitting or running.

More games can be found in Start Orienteering Book 6. Ready made sets of game cards and dominoes for symbol recognition are available from Harveys (see Appendix B), as well as packages for O-Bingo, O-Beetles, O-Snakes & Ladders and Map Drawing by Dice Throw. Harveys also supply worksheets for skills development geared to sets of overhead projector slides and maps. These can build up knowledge of maps and skills as well as being great fun.

3 MATCHING SYMBOL SHUTTLE RELAY

Practical in the gymnasium/hall

Lay out the matching sets of cards on benches, one set at each end of the gymnasium. The children write numbers 1-10 on a piece of paper. Give each child a number between 1 and 10. That is the card they start with.

The game is to run between the two benches matching the symbols and putting letters to numbers on the paper they are carrying.

Announce the rules:
   • No touching the cards
   • One number/letter at a time
   • The winner is the one to get all the cards correct in the fastest time

Increase the distance between the benches or play the game outside to increase the distance to run. Aim for about 5 minutes continuous running. More than one set of cards may be needed. Half the class running at one time might be preferable.

Practical in pairs

Half the class plays the game while their partners watch, counting the number of times their partner runs back to the first bench.

Time how long it takes them to match all the numbers and letters

Partners sit down when one has finished. When all the first half has finished, repeat with the second half.

Start again, and see if they can perform faster the second time starting with a different number. Or write down the letters A-J and run to match the numbers.

Repetition here will contribute to more sustained exercise.

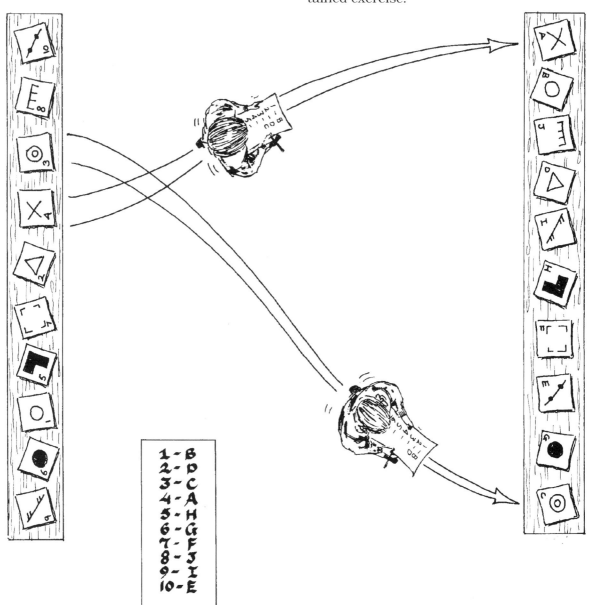

1 - B
2 - D
3 - C
4 - A
5 - H
6 - G
7 - F
8 - J
9 - I
10 - E

8 Orienteering Beyond the School

Orienteering offers a variety of experiences outside school both as a competitive sport and as recreational relaxation. This chapter contains details of opportunities. This is not exhaustive but hopefully will give a flavour of orienteering as an absorbing pastime which can extend classroom interest into enthusiasm for the Great Outdoors.

The resource section in Appendix B contains further sources of information, equipment suppliers, and details of books and manuals, including 'Teaching Orienteering', which offers a comprehensive guide for teachers.

The BSOA, BOF Schools Development Officers and most of the 150 BOF specialist orienteering clubs are able to offer mapping and competitive help to local schools. Many club-school links exist which help children into the mainstream competition system. Schools can affiliate to BOF through BSOA or directly to their local club or region. - and thereby receive information and guidance. Parents can be an important resource in developing children's interest outside school under specialist teacher guidance. Other fruitful partnerships have been built up with Outdoor Education Centres, local Sports Development Officers, Regional Councils of Sport and Disability Organisations. Community links bring advantages to both sides, not least in access to suitable orienteering terrain.

PERMANENT COURSES

Permanent courses are the orienteering equivalent of running tracks or sports halls. They offer a valuable resource for school, club and community coaching and training.

Essentially, a permanent course is a scatter of marker posts set in a park, wood or forest section and shown by the usual numbered circles on an orienteering map. Some urban maps may be simple in the extreme and the courses may require the participants to weave between fences or buildings. Forestry Commission Courses sometimes still use the term "Wayfaring" and show runnable forest as green on the map instead of white. The posts are usually moved at regular intervals to avoid the

creation of a new path network between controls.

Used imaginatively, permanent courses can offer much more than a score type introduction to orienteering, but like all sports halls they require experienced and qualified coaches and leaders to bring out their full potential as an orienteering resource. Many of the exercises in this Teacher Guide can be used on permanent courses and we also list the following which are particularly effective, in that they save 'teacher' energy and time in setting out and retrieving markers as well as giving control of the activity.

- Controls can be permutated for introductory handrail courses
- Star exercises for team competitions or compass exercises
- Team or individual score events
- Compass and distance judgement exercises
- Relocation exercises
- Pairs exercises

Most of these exercises can give technical and physical training even where the area is well known to the participants. A school programme, involving all the ideas mentioned above, could realistically be planned and carried out on one permanent course. A comprehensive list of permanent courses in the UK is available from the British Orienteering National Office. This includes contact addresses and map outlets.

COLOUR CODED EVENTS

Colour Coded Events are cross-country orienteering competitions intended to cater for all levels of orienteering ability. Courses are designated by colour, where each colour represents a course with a certain level of physical and technical difficulty (generally the darker the colour the longer or harder the course). This ensures a consistency of course standards between events so that someone entering an Orange course one weekend will be able to enter an Orange Course the following weekend in a different area confident that the physical and technical standards will be similar.

A youngster is expected to start on either the White or Yellow course, whilst an adult novice begins with either the Yellow, Orange or Red course, depending on his or her confidence. Progression can then be made either towards longer courses with the navigation remaining relatively simple, or onto technically difficult courses up to the appropriate length for the individual's level of fitness.

The shorter courses with a low level of technical difficulty (White and Yellow) will be mainly along paths so the terrain and technical difficulty will have only a small effect on competitors' times. More difficult courses will demand compass, route choice and contour skills and could involve steep climbs and rough terrain. The level of difficulty will influence guidelines on time.

Colour awards

A White Award can be made to anyone who completes three White courses.

The Colour Coded Standard for courses other than White is either the time that is achieved by at least 50% of those who started the course (including the retirals and disqualifications), or 150% of the winner's time - whichever gives the largest number of qualifiers. The Controller has discretion to extend the qualifying time, but not to reduce it.

A competitor qualifies for a colour award (other than White) by attaining the Colour Coded Standard for that course on three separate occasions.

Pairs can qualify for colour awards on the White, Yellow and Orange courses. Most BOF regions and clubs issue badges or certificates for those who achieve awards.

Ambitious schools and motivated pupils who wish to progress further up the mainstream competition ladder within the British Orienteering Federation Structure can enter Badge Events (see page 70) as well as National and Championship competitions. The BOF National Office can provide a full fixture list as well as details of Regional Associations and local clubs which can help schools with entry and introductory advice.

There are also over 30 schools leagues and similar schools-centred competitions nation-wide organised by the BSOA and local Schools Associations. An annual British Schools Championship which is team based takes place at different venues round the British Isles every November and regularly attracts over 1000 entrants covering 8 age classes from 10-18 for both boys and girls. This is complemented by a British Schools Score Championship in October and a Trail 'O' Championship for children with disabilities.

Schools' Incentive Schemes include the BSOA Explorer Challenge for which youngsters collect controls in events to achieve graded awards. The Young Navigator Star Award is run in conjunction with the National Navigation Award Scheme in which children work to reach competence levels on school sites for bronze, silver or gold badges and certificates. Once again BOF National Office or BSOA Office can provide details (addresses/phone nos. in Appendix B).

Colour Coded Course Guidelines

Time (mins) for most competitors	15-35	24-45	35-60	45-75	55-90	65-105	75-120
Length (km)	1.0-1.5	1.5-2.5	2.5-3.5	3.5-5.0	5.0-7.5	7.5+	10.0+
Technical difficulty / Control sites — Physical difficulty	1	2	3	3	4	5	5
1 — Major line features and junctions	White						
2 — Line features and very easy adjacent features		Yellow					
3 — Line features + easy point features close to lines			Orange	Red			
4 — Minor line and easy point features			Light Green				
5 — Small point + contour features				Green	Blue	Brown	Black

In National Curriculum terms, key stages 1 and 2 would equate to competition at white and yellow badge standard covering technical levels 1 and 2. Key stage 3 could take pupils through to Orange at level 3, and key stage 4 progresses from Orange through to Green at levels 4 and 5.

THE STEP SYSTEM

Level	Step	Skills	Techniques	Colour	Age
5+	O	Longer distances from and/or indistinct attack points & catching features		Brown + Blue	18A
5	N	Long legs (1km+)		Green	16A 18B
	M	Use complex contours; generalise contour detail			
	L	Use simple contour shapes for most/all of leg			
4	K	Use simple contour shapes over short distances on their own or with other information for longer distances	Reading contours	Light Green	14A 16B
	J	Fine orienteering on short legs	Pacing		
	I	Navigate long legs (0.6-1km) on rough compass bearing against catching features	Bearings, catching features		
3	H	Make simple route choices	Route choice	Red	12A 14B
	G	Simplification of legs with several 'decision points'	Attack points, absolute distance judgement (eg 100m along)	Orange	
	F	Orienteer over short distances against catching features	Compass directions		
	E	Cutting corners	Aiming off		
2	D	Leave a line feature to go to a visible control site, then return to it	Catching features, distance judgement (eg halfway between)	Yellow	10A 12B
	C	Orienteer along obvious line features (handrails). Decisions at 'decision points' without the aid of a control to identify it as such	Check points		
1	B	Orienteer along tracks and paths. Decisions at 'decision points' identified by control points	Thumbing, handrails	White	10B
	A	Understand map colours and commonly used symbols. Orientate the map using compass and the terrain	Folding the map		
Ground level		Understand the map, get used to being in woods		String	

At each level the sequence of development is:

1 Master the individual steps

2 Learn to select and apply the correct technique when just one technique is required

3 Learn to select and apply the correct technique when more than one is required

4 Adjust speed to the technical difficulty of the orienteering

5 Develop relocation techniques appropriate to the skill level

CHECKLIST FOR ORGANISING AN ORIENTEERING EVENT

1 Choose an appropriate area and get written permission for access. Draw up budget if appropriate.

2 The map - check scale, detail, accuracy.

3 Plan armchair course(s), then check on the ground. Arrange for a second opinion to control the event. Tape control points.

4 Choose an organisation team of adequate experience - start, finish, results computation and display.

5 Equipment: markers, punches, control cards start/finish signs, taped finish, tent, tables, results display.

6 Safety procedures
Establish and communicate to organisation team and competitors.

7 Prepare master maps (or overprint course on maps), map corrections, control description sheets. Any other instructions.

8 Set out course well in advance and have it checked by controller. Arrange for dismantling and clearing up afterwards.

9 Debrief and send out results.

10 Prepare for next event.

Orienteering organisation eats up time - plan every stage well in advance.

For schools and local events, pupils can be given organisational roles at every level except event organiser and controller, including preparation of the map.

SAFETY CODE FOR ORGANISERS OF ORIENTEERING EVENTS

Orienteering is not especially hazardous (DES Safety in Outdoor Education booklet).

1 Build safety into course planning:
Suitable area, collecting features, handrails check points, clearly marked out-of-bounds areas.

2 Participants and organisers:
Must have the right degree of experience and knowledge of maps and basic navigation techniques. Beginners take part in pairs, each individual having a map.

3. Retirement procedure:
Everyone must know it, so put it on the control description sheet - with a time limit.

4 Start and finish manned throughout by a responsible adult:
Match all finishing competitors' control cards with stubs from the start to ensure everyone is back.

5. Emergency system:
Whistle; watch; time limit; systematic pre-planned search system; safety bearings (if appropriate); First Aid.
EVERYONE MUST KNOW.

6 Ensure adequate equipment for conditions:
Protection against cold, wind and rain. Stout footwear with grip, gloves if cold, drinks if hot, map cases, etc.

ABOVE ALL . . . .

7 The difficulty of each course must be appropriate to the age, skills, fitness and experience of the participants.

9 Developing Personal Performance

BOF COACHING STRUCTURE
The British Orienteering Federation's Coaching Award Scheme is designed to help orienteers of all ages and levels of ability to realise their full potential through a uniform system of instruction, and thereby enhance their enjoyment of the sport. The scheme is divided into four levels, plus a *Teacher/Leader* award forming a basic ground level. This award qualifies staff to conduct orienteering on a named site but is not assessed.

Level 1: Instructor
The award is aimed at teachers, youth leaders, outdoor activity instructors and any others involved in introducing orienteering, mainly to young people.

Level 2: Club Coach
This coach works with beginners and less experienced orienteers of all ages at club level.

Level 3: Regional Coach
The coach is involved with personal performance at regional and national level, trains and assesses candidates for level 1 and 2 awards.

Level 4: Senior Coach
The holder of this award is an expert in orienteering who may have responsibility for a specific area of coaching at national level. He/she contributes to the running of courses, National Squad coaching,the development of coaching techniques and the generation and dissemination of coaching ideas.

Full qualification and assessment conditions for each level of award as well as the Teacher/ Leader award can be obtained from the BOF National Office. Detailed information on coaching, physical training and orienteering techniques is contained in the Federation's Training and Coaching book 'The Complete Orienteering Manual'. The Federation's coaching activities are co-ordinated by a full-time Director of Coaching, who has responsibility for part-time National Coaches who fill specific posts within the scheme. Two part-time Schools Development Officers deal with schools'

orienteering and liaise with the BSOA. A full-time English Development Officer oversees general grassroots development and promotion of the sport.

69

Incentive schemes are an important part of the sport and exist at different levels. The colour coded system has succeeded in combining competition of graded technical and physical difficulty with cheap on-the-day entry for all levels of competition at local events.

The national 'Badge' scheme awards iron, bronze, silver, gold and championship badges after three events have been completed within a time based on the average of the first three in each class, e.g. gold = average of first three +25%, silver = average of first three + 50%, etc.

The BSOA and the Scottish Orienteering Association run a scheme where badges and certificates can be gained after collecting controls at the appropriate number of timed events. This has proved an excellent scheme for beginners.

The National Navigation Award uses orienteering skills as the basis of a progressive navigation badge scheme. It includes the Young Navigator Star Award Scheme which caters for primary school children and can be operated entirely on a school site.

A full fixture list and details of incentive schemes are available from the BOF National Office or BSOA Office. The fixture list is included in CompassSport and in a quarterly BOF News which is sent to all Federation members. BSOA has its own magazine, *Search*, which provides a similar information service for schools

Competitions and incentive schemes are designed to provide the motivation for individuals to improve their orienteering techniques and overall personal competence. The figure above shows a personal performance ladder and indicates the route to the top for the ambitious orienteer.

Supporting the growth and development of personal competence is a National and Junior Squad structure and a comprehensive coaching scheme.

The Senior Squad aims directly at preparation for World Championships and, with the help of Sports Council funds, provides a programme of home and overseas courses and competitions tailored to the short and long term plans of individual members, each of whom has a personal coach.

The Junior section of the Squad seeks to identify outstanding young orienteers in Britain and to develop their technical ability so as to provide a foundation of good orienteers upon which Britain's international programme can be built.

Home competition programmes and overseas links and training camps have produced a dramatic improvement in the performance of both junior and senior teams.

Twelve regional squads cater for juniors with potential who wish to develop their skills and physical fitness. These squads, catering for the 13-17 age groups and open to gifted school pupils as well as club juniors, organise weekend courses and in some cases overseas training.

The personal performance ladder

Rung 6	The Top	**World Championships** Strengths and weaknesses • psychological factors • peaking and periodisation
Rung 5	Getting there	**National Squad,** international training camps (home/abroad), international competition 'O' strategies • balance of speed and certainty
Rung 4	Aiming high	**Regional Squad** Compass and pacing • relocation • refinement of techniques • a year plan
Rung 3	National Badge	**National & Badge events, Championships** Contours, route choice • planned physical and technical training • working hard at club coaching sessions
Rung 2	Collecting 'Colours' .	**Colour Coded events** Use of handrails • simple route choice • introduction to the compass • helped by club coaching
Rung 1	Getting started	**Club, School, Outdoor Centre** Understanding the map as a picture • orientating the map to the ground

APPENDIX A

Classroom and School maps

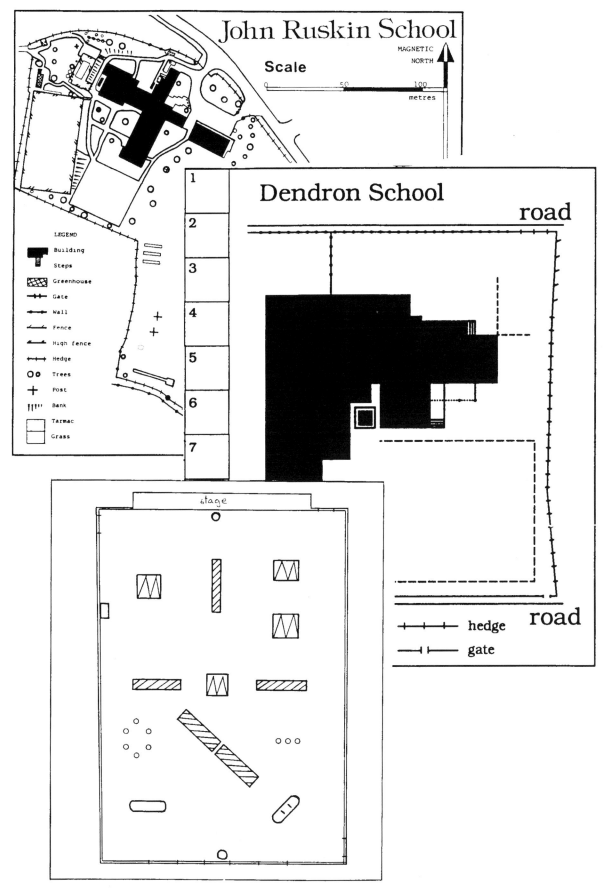

School and Park maps

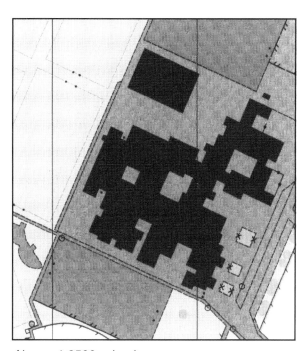

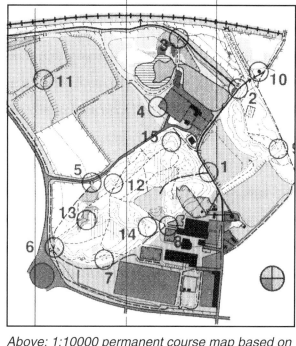

Above: 1:2500 school map
Below: 1:10000 permanent course map

Above: 1:10000 permanent course map based on a school. Below: 1:5000 park map

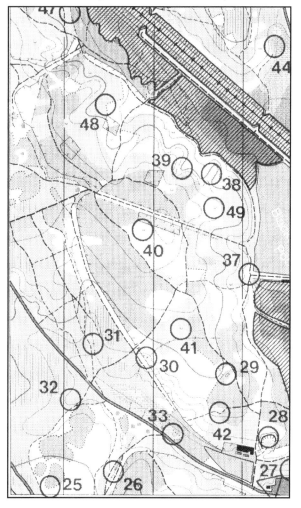

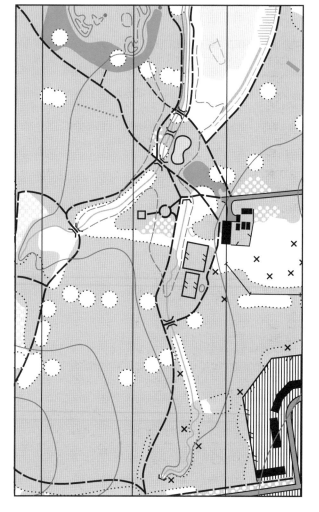

APPENDIX B   Resources for Teachers and Instructors

BOOKS AND VIDEOS

TEACHING ORIENTEERING
by Carol McNeill, Jean Ramsden, Tom Renfrew (Harveys). NEW FULLY REVISED 1997. Comprehensive manual containing over 100 lesson plans. ISBN 1 85137 020X

START ORIENTEERING
by Carol McNeill and Tom Renfrew (Harveys). A series of books of lesson plans for teachers.
Book 1 (6-8 year olds) ISBN 1 85137 0404
Book 2 (8-9 year olds) ISBN 1 85137 0501
Book 3 (9-10 year olds) ISBN 1 85137 0331
Book 4 (10-12 year olds) ISBN 1 85137 0609
Book 6 Games ISBN 1 85137 0803

ORIENTEERING IN THE NATIONAL CURRICULUM
by Carol McNeill, Jim Martland, Peter Palmer (Harveys) second edition 1998

KEY STAGES 3/4 IN THE NATIONAL CURRICULUM
by Carol McNeill, Peter Palmer (Harveys) 1993

ORIENTEERING TECHNIQUE from Start to Finish
by Bertil Norman and Arne Yngstrom (IOF)

GUIDELINES FOR COURSE PLANNING
(International Orienteering Federation)

LEARNING ORIENTEERING STEP BY STEP
G. Hasselstrand (IOF)

TRAIL ORIENTEERING (for the disabled)
by Anne Braggins (BOF) 1995

ORIENTEERING FOR THE YOUNG
by Carol McNeill, Peter Palmer & Tom Renfrew (IOF) 1993

SKILLS OF THE GAME - ORIENTEERING
by Carol McNeill (Crowood Press)
ISBN 1 85223 5586

ORIENTEERING: PATHWAYS TO EXCELLENCE
by Peter Palmer (Harveys) 1995

ORIENTEERING RULES AND GUIDELINES
British Orienteering Federation 1992

THE COMPLETE ORIENTEERING MANUAL
edited by Peter Palmer (Crowood Press)

MAPMAKING FOR ORIENTEERS
by Robin Harvey (Harveys)
ISBN 1 85137 0013

DEVELOPING NAVIGATIONAL SKILLS using the Silva Direct Compass
by Jim Martland and Sue Walsh,
- a new manual containing 100 exercises and games for compass use with and without maps (Coachwise NCF) 1993

VIDEOS:

ORIENTEERING - THE FIRST STEPS
ORIENTEERING - GOING FOR IT
TRAIL ORIENTEERING
(Mike Pearson 1995/6)

ORGANISATIONS AND AWARD SCHEMES

BRITISH ORIENTEERING FEDERATION,
Riversdale, Dale Road North, Darley Dale, Matlock, DE4 2JB. Tel: 01629 734042 (24-hour ansaphone). Fax: 01629 733769 BOF has two part time Schools Development Officers and offers introductory packs for individuals, clubs and schools, information on membership, permanent courses, coaching awards including a teacher/leader award, courses for teachers, schools schemes and fixtures. A limited number of videos are available on loan. A quarterly BOF News is sent to all members and affiliated organisations. A Coaching Newsletter is issued at regular intervals to all coaches who qualify through the BOF Coaching Award Scheme.

BRITISH SCHOOLS ORIENTEERING ASSOCIATION
BSOA Office: Peter Palmer, 2 Greenway Park Lane, Brocton, Stafford ST17 0TS
The BSOA exists to promote and develop all forms of schools orienteering. It provides fixture lists of schools events nationwide, discounted schools starter packs, a network of regional contacts, advice and help on starting and developing orienteering in school, as well as advice on mapping services, resource information and details of BOF teacher training qualifications and courses. A regular newsletter keeps affiliated schools in touch with new ideas, competition and training opportunities and with each other.

BSOA maintains very close links with BOF and the mainstream sport at club, regional and national level and with the international scene via the International Schools Sport Federation. Affiliation to BSOA gives automatic rights for a school's pupils to enter local BOF events up to and including Badge Standard events and provides opportunities to link with local clubs for access to orienteering terrain and maps and support for the entry of of promising youngsters into the mainstream sport.

Affiliation includes the cost of the Newsletter and access to discounted starter equipment packs, videos and so on.

International Orienteering Federation,
Radiokatu 20, FI-000934 Slu, Finland
The IOF Scientific Group produces a twice yearly research journal as well as publications on the previous pages. The IOF also publishes a magasine 'Orienteering World' with news of international developments.

National Coaching Foundation:
4, College Close, Beckett Park, Leeds.
Tel: 01532 744802
The NCF provides specific and non-specific sports information, resources and courses for coaches and teachers.

Resources for Teachers and Instructors (cont.)

ORGANISATIONS AND AWARDS (CONT.)

Royal Institute of Navigation
1 Kensington Gore, London SW7 2AT.
Tel: 0171 589 5021. Fax: 0171 823 8671.
The Royal Institute runs an annual Young
Navigator competition open to all schools and
ages of school children, which offers an
impressive array of prizes and which can be
tackled as a group or individual project.

National Navigation Award Scheme
The NNAS offers a 3 level Incentive Scheme
for all ages and abilities including a Young
Navigator Star Award which is teacher-
validated and can be tackled on school site.
Badges and certificates are awarded for 3
levels - bronze to gold.

Young Navigator
STAR AWARD

Achieved by

of
[School or Group]

Level achieved

Presented by

Date:-   [Chairman]

On behalf of
BRITISH SCHOOLS ORIENTEERING ASSOCIATION
AND
NATIONAL NAVIGATION AWARD SCHEME

Youth Sports Trust
Tel: 0171 321 0611 or 01509 228293
Fax: 01509 210851
The Youth Sports Trust provides 'Top Outdoors'. This is a 25 card teaching scheme for
Outdoor and Adventurous Activities within
the curriculum which includes 9 cards on
orienteering and offers additional guidance on
suitable activities for children with physical
and mental disabilities. The scheme comes
into operation in January 1999 and further
details are available from telephone enquiries
as above.

EQUIPMENT, SERVICES, MAGAZINES

Harveys: Main St, Doune, Perthshire, FK16 6BJ.
Tel: 01786 841202. Fax: 01786 841098
• Largest supplier of teaching resources,
materials, books, videos; introductory packs;
technique training worksheets; equipment
for organising orienteering.
• Mapmaking service.
• Free catalogue available.

Ultrasport: The Square, Newport, Salop, TF10 7AG.
Tel: 01952 813918
Orienteering clothing, equipment and shoes.
Ultrasport offers discounts for club and school
group orders.

Silva UK Ltd: Unit 10 Sky Business Park, Eversley
Way, Egham, Surrey, TW20 8RF
Tel: 01784 471721
Silva offer orienteering equipment and the full
range of world renowned Silva compasses,
including the new Direct compass designed
especially for school use. Discounts are
available for club and school group orders.

Orienteering Services (Martin Bagness)
2 Gale Crescent, Lower Gale, Ambleside LA22
0BD. Tel:019394 34184.
Map survey and drawing, instruction/coaching
for orienteering courses at all levels

Compass Sport: 37 Sandycoombe Road,
Twickenham, Middlesex, TW1 2LR.
Magazine for orienteers, 8 issues per annum.
Subscriptions: 25 The Hermitage, Eliot Hill
London SE13 7EH. Tel: 0181 852 1457

APPENDIX C   Glossary of Common Orienteering Terms

Aiming off - to aim deliberately to one side of a control on a line feature so that you know which way to turn on hitting the feature before seeing the control.

Attack Point - an obvious feature near a control point from which the control can be located by navigating carefully with map and compass.

Bearing - the direction of travel by compass.

BOF - British Orienteering Federation

Catching Feature - an obvious feature on map and ground beyond a control which can be used for relocation if the control is missed.

Check Point - an obvious feature on map and ground which can be used to check that you are keeping to your chosen route.

Collecting Feature - a feature beside a route which can be used to simplify navigation and 'contain' any diversion from the correct route.

Colour Coded System - an incentive scheme in which colours represent degrees of technical and physical difficulty thus allowing competitions to progress in skill and personal performance. Badges can be awarded for success at each level.

Contour Only Maps - reprints or photocopies of the brown printing plate for a map which show only ground shape and no other detail.

Control - a trapezoid marker (usually orange and white) used to mark features on an orienteering course - usually with clipper or punch attached to mark a control card as proof of visit.

Course - a sequence of control points marked on map and ground which have to be visited in a given order in an orienteering event.

Direct Compass - simplified Silva Protractor Compass for schools and introductory use.

Dog Leg - positioning of a control which allows competitors to go in and leave it by the same route thereby leading other competitors to it.

Fartlek - a Swedish word for enjoyable running with impromptu fast and slow sections.

Fight - an area of thick vegetation or forest through which it is difficult to pass - shown as dark green on an orienteering map.

Fine Orienteering - precision navigation in detailed terrain usually demanding careful use of map, compass and pacing and usually involving short legs.

Handrail - a line feature on map and ground followed to simplify navigation.

Leg - a section of a course between two control points.

Legend or **Key** - a list of the symbols represented on the map.

Line Event - a course in which the competitor follows a line on the map. A useful exercise for map contact.

Master Maps - maps near the start from which competitors have to copy their course.

Map Memory - a course in which competitors (without maps) have to memorise each individual leg from map sections shown at control points.

Map Guide Compass - a Silva 'Clip-On' compass which allows the map to be orientated to magnetic north very simply with map and compass together.

Orientating a Map - matching map to terrain so that north on the map points to north on the ground - sometimes called 'setting' or 'aligning'.

Pace Counting - a system of counting double paces to check off distance covered over the ground. It can be translated to a scale on the leading edge of a compass.

Permanent Course - a course with permanent markers and edge of a compass overprinted maps for recreational use.

Pre-marked Map - one with the course overprinted on it which is normally given out to the competitor at the start.

Glossary of Common Orienteering Terms (cont.)

Pre-start - call up time, usually 1-3 minutes before the start.

Protractor Compass - the conventional Silva type compass in which a movable housing on a transparent base plate with direction arrow is used to take bearings.

Relocation - finding yourself when lost.

Ride - a grassy or rough linear break between trees.

Rough Orienteering - fast navigation on easy sections of a course using rough compass bearings and obvious collecting features and checkpoints to keep map contact.

Score Orienteering - a competition to find as many controls as possible in any order, and in a fixed time, with penalties for lateness.

Setting the Map - orientating the map

Shadowing - a method of following orienteers on training exercises to check skills and analyse technique - often done by pairs exchanging roles.

Simplification - breaking down the navigation on each course leg into easy and difficult sections with the aid of checkpoints, collecting features and attack points.

Star Exercise - a training activity from a central start and finish point in which participants radiate out to visit one control at a time before returning to the centre.

Step System - a progression of orienteering skills starting with map familiarity at the lowest level and progressing to fine navigation at the top. It forms the basis of coaching, colour coded competitions and some childrens incentive schemes.

String Course - a course for young children marked throughout by a line of string. Children find controls without getting lost. To make it more difficult the line only cab be shown on the map upon which competitors have to mark each control accurately as they find it.

Stub - the tear-off part of the control card which is handed in at the pre-start and serves as a check on competitors out in the forest as well as being used to display results.

Thumbing - using your thumb to mark your location on a folded map.

Thumb Compass - a compass which clips to the thumb of the map hand allowing easy map orientation and direction finding, but not accurate bearings.

Vegetation Boundary - the line between two distinct types of vegetation shown by a dotted line on maps.

Walk Forest - an area of dense trees where running speed is much reduced.

APPENDIX D
Intra-Curricular Orienteering - PE Outdoor and Adventurous Activity. Key Stages 2/3

OBJECTIVES
- *to teach navigation skills*
- *to solve simple navigational problems on and off site*
- *to compete in orienteering activities individually and as a team*
- *to develop runnung activity to improve cardio-vascular fitness*
- *to assess personal performance*

SUGGESTED PROGRAMME for 7x1hour sessions based on a selection of lesson plans

TIME	ACTIVITY	SKILLS	EQUIPMENT
Week 1	Explain the concept of a map, legend and scale. Draw own map of classroom or gym with furniture arranged as 'forest'. Use the map to explain and demonstrate orientation. Plan own courses, put out mini- markers, walk or run courses with orientated maps following lines as handrails.	Map reading Orientation without compass Handrails	Paper Pencils Mini-markers or streamers
Week 2	Map walk with **site map** - explaining legend and scale - relate to distance on ground. Pace 100m and relate back to map. Stress handrail technique again. Pupils complete loop courses between controls on site - using control cards and punches if possible, eg 4 loops of about 400m each permutating 12 control points.	Handrails Legend Scale	Site map Control cards Punches, or pencils to write down code letters Control markers
Week 3	Introduce the **compass** - explain the principle and working. Orientate the site map with the compass. Compasss exercise on the field, eg running directions and distance.	Compass	Site map Compasses
Week 4	a) Pupils put out a scatter of 20 controls on site using prepared map, eg one control each in pairs. b) A score event - 20 min to get as many points as possible - penalty deduction if late.	Map reading & orientation a) with partner b) individually, own decisions	Pre-marked site map Control markers Compasses?
Week 5	Relays on site map: a) Teams of 3 - each runner does a different loop - A, B, C, or b) Cloverleaf with mass start - first complete team back, the winner or c) Scatter of 20 controls - teams of 3 decide who in each team gets which contols.	Map reading on the run Map orientation Working in a team	Pre-marked site map Control markers Punches? Compasses?
Week 6	Transfer to local park [Repeat week 2 or 4 exercises (Loops or Score event)] Pupils can put out a control each if area is suitable, or work in pairs. They can also follow a line marked on the map, punching as they come across controls, or mark where they are on the map - if pupils are not on the line they will miss the controls.	Transference of skills to unfamiliar terrain Line event - close contact with map	Pre-marked park map Control markers Punches? Compasses Whistles? Bibs?
Week 7	Competitive event in the local park starting at one minute intervals on 2km course with about 10 control points. If possible involve the group in organisation of an event - start, timekeeping, results, etc. Produce a results list, etc.	Revision of all previous work Can be used for assessment Organisation skills	Park map, pre-marked or master maps Control markers Punches? Whistles? Compasses. Bibs?

If no local park is available outside school, other site activities could include:
- Punching Relay - visiting controls in limited area. Team punch and run as quickly as possible with penalties for punches outside the 'box'.
- Indoor - relay transferring course from map at one end of hall to blank map at other end - master map practice.
- 'O' Bingo, Harveys map/symbol cards, worksheets - all in the classroom.
- Map drawing competition - the best sketch map of a small area drawn in 20 mins - used for a small mini-competition.

APPENDIX E

Making an Orienteering Map

A good accurate map is essential if orienteering is to be done properly. There are many professional and part-time mapmakers, but if funds are short it is possible to 'do it yourself'. Map making can be fun, the children can be involved and it is rewarding to see others orienteering on your map.

There are four stages in making a simple map
- finding a map to use as a base
- doing the fieldwork to add detail which can be used for orienteering
- transforming fieldwork notes into artwork suitable for reproduction
- producing black & white or colour copies

Base map

The first stage in producing a simple orienteering map is usually to find an existing map to use as a base. If the intention is to make a map of a school grounds, a copy of an Ordnance Survey map is probably the easiest route to take. An architects' plan may be an option - there may be an overall site plan at a scale suitable for an orienteering map (1:1000-1:2500). When making a map of a park or woodland, an OS map is usually the only accurate material available.

OS maps are published at various scales. There are 1:2500 maps of urban areas. The 1:10000 map is rather small scale for this kind of map but this is the largest OS scale that includes contour information.

Remember that to copy any map, permission must be obtained from the copyright holder (who may make a charge). See p80 for the BOF/OS scheme.

If the base material is not at the scale you wish to use, enlargement or reduction is most cheaply done on a photocopier.

Fieldwork

The next stage is to take the base map and make any changes required. This involves adding new detail and reclassifying features already on the map to an orienteering specification. Exactly what to include on a map will vary from area to area. A look at similar maps is the best guide to what is needed.

For fieldwork the materials needed are:
- a copy of the base map

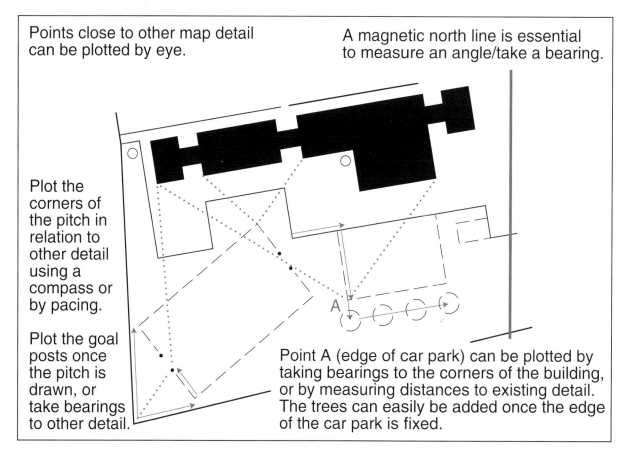

Points close to other map detail can be plotted by eye.

A magnetic north line is essential to measure an angle/take a bearing.

Plot the corners of the pitch in relation to other detail using a compass or by pacing.

Plot the goal posts once the pitch is drawn, or take bearings to other detail.

Point A (edge of car park) can be plotted by taking bearings to the corners of the building, or by measuring distances to existing detail. The trees can easily be added once the edge of the car park is fixed.

- drawing film. This is waterproof, stable and can be laid over the base map for tracing.
- a protractor compass
- a hard pencil and coloured crayons

Two skills are needed - using a protractor compass and pace counting. The positioning of new detail is done either with a compass (for direction) or pacing (for distance), or a combination of both. In a school environment all new detail can often be plotted simply by taking distance measurements, without getting involved with compass bearings. To measure distances, you will need to practise a metre pace length or know how to convert your normal pacing to metres. Some form of measuring tape is necessary to mark out a sample distance to measure your pacing against.

To plot a line accurately using a compass, the base map must have magnetic north lines for reference. Without a grid line to help magnetic north is best worked out as follows (north arrows on architects' plans are often inaccurate):

- Take a bearing (b) along an existing straight line on the map (edge of building or road).
- Set an angle of (360 - b)° on the compass.
- Rotate the whole compass until the lines on the base of the *housing* are parallel with the line of the feature on the map.
- A line now drawn along the edge of the base plate will be magnetic north.

A combination of plotting angles and measuring distances will allow you to fix the position of any objects in the area. Anything which is distinct on the ground can be shown on a simple orienteering map. Be careful not to include too much detail or the map will be difficult to read.

Look at map legends or symbol lists to see how features on the ground should be classified to make your map an orienteering map.

It is good practice to produce a clean copy of all the detail to be included on the map. This is best done by putting an overlay over the base map and (a) tracing the existing detail to be retained and (b) adding new detail that has been surveyed. A polyester drawing film is the best material for the overlay.

If this draft is drawn carefully it can be used as the master for photocopying without any further work.

Artwork

There are a number of options for transforming fieldwork results into a map ready for use.

PHOTOCOPYING/HAND COLOURING

A well drawn survey draft can be copied and used in black and white, or hand coloured. Alternatively the original draft could be hand coloured if there is access to a colour copier.

Try to keep the map to an A4 size if photocopying. Within this restraint keep the scale figure a round number if possible (eg 1:2500)

HAND DRAWING

Traditional artwork for a colour map involves hand drawing separate overlays in black ink for each colour to be printed.

Lines are drawn with special drawing pens with different nibs giving different line thicknesses. Point symbols are either drawn with a pen or applied from dry transfer (rub-on) sheets. Areas/patterns are applied by cutting shapes from sheets of self adhesive film.

All these materials are available from specialist orienteering mapmaking suppliers.

Hand drawing is still an option, of course, but the advent of computers in schools has overshadowed this method.

COMPUTER DRAWING

If the teacher or the class has access to a computer with suitable software the map could be drawn as part of the classroom activities. A simple drawing programme is all that is needed for a school map. Such a programme must be able to do a number of things:

- draw a line and colour it. The possibility of drawing curved lines is preferable but a curved line can be a series of short straight lines if necessary.
- draw shapes and colour them.
- change the orientation of lines and objects.

Even simple drawing programmes can usually do more than this. After a short time the children will be more expert than the teacher!

There is an orienteering map drawing programme called OCAD. This is relatively inexpensive and widely used throughout the orienteering world.

The first step is to get the information from the draft map on the computer. There are

options depending on the availability of equipment:
• to scan the draft and have it on screen as a template to trace over.
• to use a digitising tablet.
• to transfer information by eye/measurement - a grid drawn on the draft and on the screen is the starting stage.

MAP LAYOUT
The design of a map should include various items of information:

• the map itself
• title, and logos if required
• scale, scale bar, (contour interval if relevant)
• key to all the symbols used
• magnetic north lines
• credits to copyright owners, disclaimers, etc.

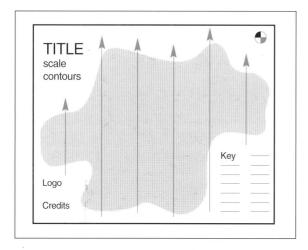

BOF has an agreement with the OS for using their maps as a base. The map must bear a credit with specific wording and a licence number - *Based upon the Ordnance Survey mapping with the permission of Her Majesty's Stationery Office. © Crown Copyright. Licence no. . . . . . .* Consult BOF Office for details.

Reproduction
If number of copies required is small, producing the artwork on computer gives the greatest flexibility. It is relatively cheap to run off colour copies as required. Amendments can be made very quickly and new copies produced. Copies can be mounted or heatsealed for repeated use.

If hand drawing or if a large number of copies is required, commercial colour printing of a map will be the cheapest option. It also gives a higher quality of print. Consultation with a printer or mapmaking company at the outset is essential if problems are to be avoided.

Detailed advice is given in *Mapmaking for Orienteers* - see appendix B).